Rice Wine with the Minister

Rice Wine with the Minister

Distilled Wisdom to Manage, Lead and Succeed on the Global Stage

Andrew Kakabadse
Professor of International Management Development,
Cranfield School of Management,
Cranfield University, UK

Nada Kakabadse
Professor in Management and Business Research,
Northampton Business School, UK

First published 2010 by
PALGRAVE MACMILLAN

Palgrave Macmillan in the UK is an imprint of Macmillan Publishers Limited, registered in England, company number 785998, of Houndmills, Basingstoke, Hampshire RG21 6XS.

Palgrave Macmillan in the US is a division of St Martin's Press LLC, 175 Fifth Avenue, New York, NY 10010.

Palgrave Macmillan is the global academic imprint of the above companies and has companies and representatives throughout the world.

Palgrave® and Macmillan® are registered trademarks in the United States, the United Kingdom, Europe and other countries.

ISBN 978-0-230-23295-2

This book is printed on paper suitable for recycling and made from fully managed and sustained forest sources. Logging, pulping and manufacturing processes are expected to conform to the environmental regulations of the country of origin.

A catalogue record for this book is available from the British Library.

A catalog record for this book is available from the Library of Congress.

10 9 8 7 6 5 4 3 2 1
19 18 17 16 15 14 13 12 11 10

Printed and bound in Great Britain by
CPI Antony Rowe, Chippenham and Eastbourne

A word to the wise
The rice wine called Maotai is classified in China as "sauce" fragrance (醬香; pinyin: jiàng xiāng): "A highly fragrant distilled liquor of bold character. To the Western palate, sauce fragrance baijiu can be quite challenging."

Wikipedia

CONTENTS

Acknowledgments

Our deepest thanks to Madeleine Fleure for having prepared and adjusted script after script in such a warm, friendly, and professional manner. Thank you also to Sheena Darby for having organized numerous meetings and encounters with a large number of managers who provided us with the rich stories that are the heart and soul of this book. Sheena, your patience and good humor helped all to talk openly and freely.

Also we are deeply grateful to Stuart Crainer and Des Dearlove for their invaluable advice and editorial skill. You have both brought this book to life.

Our grateful thanks also go to Alexi Mordashov, Vadim Makhov, Dmitry Afanasyev, and Dmitry Kouptsov and the Severstal Corporation for their generous support in sponsoring the case studies in this book through the Cranfield/Severstal program.

We have not forgotten all those managers, directors, and interesting individuals who have provided the experiences, tales, and case material for this text. Not only you but there are countless others who have formed our experiences that so helped us to write this guide for the global manager.

Thank you to you all.

The starting point of this book is a life-changing encounter with rice wine. I had a similar experience one unforgettable lunchtime in 2008 with the Beijing Olympic Committee. There were smiles all round as I was plied with shot after shot, but it was clear I was being tested for something more serious than my ability to handle Maotai.

I have thought a lot about this experience since. Traditions tend to last hundreds of years if they serve a useful purpose, so why did my hosts decide that I was OK? They saw I was willing to embrace their custom. And I think they judged that the Maotai showed them the real me, even if I wasn't exactly crisp.

That lunch made its mark because it reinforced one the most important things I had learned since becoming the CEO of a global firm in 2006: the paradox of control. The perennial question is how to get others to care as much about your objectives as you do. Coercion is a constant temptation, but good leaders understand that achieving their ambitions means seeing the world through the eyes of the people they hope to influence. As you rise through an organization, your dependence on others grows in line with your theoretical power to shape events.

This conundrum has been magnified a thousand times by globalization. The traditional take on global expansion assumes centralized power, which in turn assumes that a strategist in Ohio can second-guess what is going on in the mind of a customer in Hamburg or Beijing or Dubai. Command/control is incompatible with the flexibility organizations need to compete globally. It's a philosophy which is already hopelessly out of step with our new reality, and firms which cling to it will become increasingly endangered.

Organizations struggle with this conundrum because leaders struggle with it. We regularly shoehorn the unfamiliar into parameters we can readily understand, because we find the unknown disconcerting even if it's exciting. But it's time to wean ourselves off some of the old certainties. Hofstede's cultural dimensions are still thought-provoking, but they're based on questionnaires filled out over 30 years ago by employees from one multinational: IBM. And our faith in measurement has to become more thoughtful. All organizations need to be informed by data, and there is nothing wrong per se with sales targets or shareholder value, but they persuade the unwary to look no further than the short term, the expedient, and the easily measurable. Since competitive advantage on the global stage depends on virtues like integrity and collaboration, ambitious leaders need to find ways to value them too.

The big prize for global firms is to understand that precious moment when two people from opposite sides of the world decide to trust each other. Until they truly understand it, they can't value or replicate it. All this begins with real people looking at the world with fresh eyes and trying new ways of working. As Henry Thoreau put it (that great nineteenth-century enemy of tired ideas): "How can we remember our ignorance, which our growth requires, if we use our knowledge all the time?"

So let me summarize, I have highlighted but a few reasons why "Rice Wine with the Minister" fills a crucial gap in our understanding of what it means to behave globally.

L. Kevin Kelly is Chief Executive Officer of Heidrick & Struggles, the leading global search and advisory firm. He has built leadership teams at board level across the Americas, Asia Pacific, and Europe.

Andrew Kakabadse is Professor of International Management Development, at Cranfield University's School of Management in the UK. He has held visiting appointments at the Center for Creative Leadership and at Thunderbird, The Garvin School of International Management, in the United States. Currently he is Visiting Professor at the University of Ulster in the UK; at Macquarie Graduate School of Management, Australia; at Swinburne University Institute of Technology, Australia as well as at the Pantheon-Assas, Paris. He is also a fellow at the Windsor Leadership Trust, UK. Andrew has consulted and lectured in every region of the world. His bestselling books include *The Politics of Management, Working in Organisations,* and *The Wealth Creators.* Andrew Kakabadse was born in Greece of Georgian descent and spends his time circling the globe.

Nada Kakabadse is a research professor at the University of Northampton Business School in the UK. Previously, she was a senior research fellow at the Cranfield School of Management. She has lived and worked in Scandinavia, Middle East, Australia, and Canada. She has worked for global corporations as well as the federal governments of Canada and Australia. She is co-editor of *Corporate Governance: The International Journal of Business in Society* and the *Journal of Management Development.* She is a Visiting Professor at Ulster University Business School; Macquarie Graduate School of Management, Sydney, Australia; at the University of Pantheon-Assas, Paris, France; at the Capital University of Business and Economics, Beijing, China; and at the Institute of Public Administration, Kazakhstan.

Andrew and Nada are the authors of *Leadership in Government* (1998), *Essence of Leadership* (1999), *Creating Futures: Innovative Applications of IS/IT* (2000), *The Geopolitics of Governance* (2001), *Smart Sourcing* (2002), *Intimacy: An International Survey of the Sex Lives of People at Work* (2004), *Governance, Strategy and Policy: Seven Critical Essays* (2006), *CSR in Practice: Delving Deep* (2007), *Leading the Board: The Six Disciplines of World Class Chairman* (2008), *The Elephant Hunters: Chronicles of the Moneymen* (2008; with Amielle Lake), *Leading for Success: Seven Sides to Great Leaders* (2008; with Linda Lee-Davies), *Leadership Teams: Developing and Sustaining High Performance* (2009; with Geoff Sheard), *Global Boards: One Desire, Many Realities* (2009), and *Citizenship: A Reality Far from Ideal* (2009; with Kalu N. Kalu).

Triple R Global Leader

The genesis of this book goes back to 2008 when one of the authors (Andrew) was invited to a central province of China called Hunan. Traditionally regarded as the cradle of Chinese civilization and birthplace of Mao Tse Tung, Andrew was there to act as an advisor to a multinational setting up in the area. On arriving he was introduced to the Chinese minister, and offered a refreshing, if potent, local rice wine called Maotai. This, he later learned, was the drink Zhou Enlai had used to entertain

Richard Nixon at the state banquet for the U.S. presidential visit in 1972.

No negotiations, Andrew was told, would take place until the local customs were complete. What he realized only later was that in this particular province, strangers are invited to drink shots of the local liquor to prove they are worthy to be admitted to the negotiating table. The local culture is historically based on masculinity. In antiquity the warrior who could drink and fight was presented with any number of women. This is all very well, but Maotai is 60 per cent proof and is drunk straight. No water. No ice.

Drawing on his early experiences visiting the land of his fathers, Georgia in the former Soviet Union, and his belief in the importance of breaking social barriers, Andrew drained his glass—21 times—to toast each of the people present and to acknowledge the hospitality of the hotel owner and his three sons. By still being able to walk after 21 shots of rice wine, he passed the test—unlike all the others at the table apart from the minister. Social and commercial barriers disappeared. The hangover was memorable though temporary, but the metaphor remained with him.

Since then we have observed time and time again how local culture and global leadership are entwined. Despite all the talk of the world becoming increasingly similar, no matter where you go, the reality is that every situation is different. The big message of this book is that heterogeneity rules the global roost. Every country and even every province has its own unique ways and nuances. Global citizens beware. What is regarded as unprofessional in one part of the world is a test of a leader's character in another. What is seen as corruption in one place is seen somewhere else as deep-seated familial loyalty.

But it is only by navigating the differences—and doing so in ways by which you remain true to your own values—that business leaders can operate effectively on the global stage. And when it comes to global commerce, Western leaders have as much, if not more, to learn than their Eastern counterparts.

In Rice Wine with the Minister, we try to get to the reality of global leadership, epitomized by 21 leadership lessons—or 21 shots of leadership wisdom—for today's global world.

The bazaar context

The overriding reality is that of the global arena we now operate in, for those in business, the world has never been smaller: interconnected, always open for business, largely free of trade barriers, despite the recent economic downturn—this is commercial nirvana. And yet, it often does not feel like that. Making sense of the global bazaar—and making money from it—is incredibly complex and requires a pot-pourri of skills and sensitivities. Too often these are described and constrained by what could be politely called economic rationalism. Organizations, usually Western, see the world through the blinkered perspective of shareholder value rather than the cosmopolitan technicolor of stakeholder concerns which the globalized business world deserves.

Rice Wine with the Minister provides a practical guide to the realities of leading in this truly global arena. After all, few significantly sized businesses are without international aspirations. Often the biggest stumbling block is not opportunity but leadership. The imperative to move to a truly global appreciation of, and application of, leadership is increasingly apparent.

Our conclusions on what it takes to lead on the global stage aren't the final word on the topic—no book could do that—but they are based on research and direct (sometimes headache-inducing) personal experience. Our Top Teams and Boards research is the largest international database of senior managers in the world and, over the past 20 years, we have lived and worked in more than 20 countries.

Triples all round

The model we have developed to better understand the realities of global leadership has three elements.

Reach: Some executives we encounter have limited reach. They are one-company servants who see the world through corporate-tinted lenses; functional specialists who have spent way too long in one business area. They have their way of doing things and seeing things and are resolutely unenthusiastic about exploring beyond their comfort zones. Global leaders are the antithesis. They have a constant and urgent willingness to reach beyond themselves. They reach out to embrace new experiences, knowledge, and cultures. They reach out to people no matter where they are located.

Part of the reach element of global leadership is that today's global leaders are superbly and globally networked. Their networks must embrace the stakeholders they need to engage with to help their organizations be successful. Networks link global concerns to local context. As part of their networks, leaders must have political connections to negotiate favorable terms and conditions in each of the countries where they do business.

Readiness: Being willing to run with an experience or an idea is at the heart of being a global leader. The best leaders we have encountered exhibit a perpetual state of readiness. They want to explore and are prepared to wander off-piste with a local guide. They automatically prepare the ground for their adventures. They research people and places before they meet or visit them. For them, cultural due diligence is a vital tool in being ready for business.

Roll out: Global leaders don't simply pay a visit and add exotic names to their BlackBerry's address book and wacky stories to their repertoire. They are fascinated by and driven by results, but realize that they may not come easily or quickly and that one side's interpretation of those results may differ from another's.

Reach, readiness, and roll out are the Triple Rs of global leadership. In our experience, the best global leaders display a mastery of all of these elements.

Clearly, this is a formidable task. Becoming a truly global leader is an increasingly necessary aspiration, but one that requires hard work, a level of self-awareness, capacious curiosity, and a sizeable intellect. The good news is that sensitivity to the world—and your self—can be acquired. *Rice Wine with the Minister* provides 21 pointers to what it takes to manage, lead, and succeed on the global stage.

Just as Chris Bartlett and Sumantra Ghoshal talked about the evolution toward a transnational corporation in their famous book *Managing across Borders*, so we believe there is a continuum of leadership—from regional, to national, to multinational (typically just a colonial view), to international, to transcultural or global. Understanding the issues we raise in this book—even if you don't agree with all our conclusions and observations—is vital if you are to lead any global organization.

Rice Wine with the Minister distils our experiences into something which we hope is practically useful for all those doing business internationally and for all those who will do so in the years to come.

Part I: Reach

Shot #1: Live the global paradox. The world may appear increasingly homogenous, but this is an illusion created by a lack of travel. In reality, our differences are more important than ever. The challenge is to live with the paradox rather than bulldozing a way through it.

Shot #2: Be comfortable with complexity. As the world shifts from homogeneity to heterogeneity, complexity lurks at every corner. See the opportunities in complexity. Learn to love it.

Shot #3: Redefine leadership. To lead in the global arena, you must begin by rethinking everything you know and assume about leadership.

Shot #4: Negotiate the gray areas of governance. Global leaders recognize that right and wrong can vary with context. They are able to move from black and white to multiple hues of gray. Their skill is to grasp the full spectrum of the colors of the rainbow.

Shot #5: Network like crazy ... and globally. The network is the thing. Quality of relationships and network is often more important than squeezing out cost. The challenge is to put effectiveness above efficiency. Who do you know? How far is your reach?

Part II: Readiness

Shot #6: Acquire cultural intelligence. Failure to understand a particular culture can prove expensive. The best global leaders are culturally sensitive.

Shot #7: Learn the language of business. Culture always requires the twist of context and nowhere is this more troublesome than in the use of language. Words have alternative meanings depending on where you are in the world. Handle with care.

Shot #8: Master meetings that matter. For some, a meeting is held in a formal space for a specific purpose—to discuss x or y. Others meet in a restaurant without having a designated aim—and do business. Which kind of meeting is it?

Shot #9: Be responsible for business. Corporate responsibility means taking responsibility in society. But that requires a strong sense of personal responsibility. Leadership is essential—no matter where you may be. The top man or woman is *the* role model, the arbiter of what matters and what is valued.

Shot #10: Speak up without talking down. Attitudes toward speaking out vary from place to place. Often seen as a cultural issue, it isn't so much cultural as company specific. If managers speak up then followers take their lead. Only then can all speak up. Workers of the world must be encouraged to exercise their voices.

Shot #11: Take a diverse view of diversity. In Greece, many entrepreneurs are women. In South Africa, diversity is all about race. How do you stand above the political correctness which dogs diversity? The reality is that diversity means developing talented leaders. Period.

Shot #12: Understand communication channels. Tune in to how people communicate in different places and situations. The wrong communication channel can lead to confused signals. Without clear and regular communication nothing gets done.

Shot #13: Privacy and confidentiality have very different meanings around the globe. What can and can't you say? Where and when can you say it?

Shot #14: Respond to age-old issues. In the West, older managers are regarded as past it and best pushed aside. In the East, age is revered and older managers are seen as the repositories of wisdom and brokers of power networks.

Part III: Roll Out

Shot #15: Deliver on decisions. Communicate, tune-in, understand the context, and then get buy-in. The bottom line is universal: delivery is king. Global strategy always has a local context.

Shot #16: Decide to decide. In some cultures, a decision is a decision. But elsewhere long-term relationships take precedence over today's apparently essential decision. Understand the local dynamics of decisions.

Shot #17: Play to the politics of place. In some countries managers try to draw a sharp line between business and politics. But this is a false division. Political skills are essential to getting things done—and the bigger and more complex an organization, the bigger the need for political skills. Learn to regard compromise as a positive outcome not a failure.

Shot #18: Treat people fairly. The need to feel treated fairly is universal. Across the world, people will work very long hours and be content if they feel they are treated fairly and respectfully. Key to making this a reality is how top management handle their local counterparts. Treat them fairly and the message spreads.

Shot #19: Learn as you go. Leaders need inquiring minds. Development may involve being sent on external training programs. But elsewhere development happens more naturally in the workplace and, in developing countries, external programs are prized. Willingness to learn is crucial. Always.

Shot #20: Question authority. Too much harmony can be as oppressive—and ineffective—as too much conflict. Questions matter more than answers. It is all a matter of identifying the pathways to questioning authority.

Shot #21: Understand who carries the can. Blame is not universal nor universally understood. Different cultures have a different take on who shoulders the blame when things go wrong—and who gets the plaudits when things succeed.

PART I

Reach

Triple R Global Leader

*The animal with the bigger field to graze upon
has better health and wider horizons.*

Proverb

Live the global paradox

The world may appear increasingly homogenous, but this is an illusion. In reality, our differences are more important than ever. The challenge is to live with the paradox rather than bulldozing a way through it.

The reality of globalization

Wang Jinlong, president of Starbucks' China operations, has a dream. He wants to make coffee from China as well known as Chinese tea. A new line of home-grown coffee, poetically called "South of the clouds," is now on offer at Starbucks' Chinese stores.[1] And stores there are aplenty. Visit Beijing today and you have a choice of 70 Starbucks stores for your daily frappuccino fix. "Enjoy great coffee amid the harmonious combination of Western and Chinese culture," encourages Starbucks' marketing. Sitting amid the Wi-Fi connected young Chinese with their laptops and trilling cell phones, it is harmoniously familiar. The Chinese baristas speak caffeine-centered English. Even the prices—31 yuan ($4.53) for a venti latte—are authentically Western.

Starbucks has quickly colonized the world—more than 15,000 stores now adorn 44 countries and there are still untapped markets to explore.

After their frappuccinos, Beijingers can go on to visit one of the city's Wal-Mart stores among the 100 in China. Wal-Mart now imports more than 6,600 categories of American products into China, from Californian grapes to Washington apples and popcorn. It opened 23 stores in China in 2007 alone. Around the world, the retail juggernaut has 6,500 stores in 14 markets, employs more than 1.9 million people, and serves over 179 million customers a year.

Globalization is a reality. Finance, production, marketing, technology, and virtually all business relationships and arrangements criss-cross borders.

And it works. Globalization has changed the world's politics, its economics, its cultures. Generally, it has done so for the greater good. The process of globalization led to the unification of Germany, the break-up of the Soviet Union, the formation of trading blocks (such as NAFTA and ASEAN), frappuccinos in unlikely places, and much more.

There is no escape from the process of globalization and its implications in your life and your working life. Globalization has created opportunities for CEOs from BRIC economies to become global entrepreneurs. Think of the rise of Tata, Mittal, and Petro China. It took the Indian company Infosys 23 years to reach $1 billion in revenues and just another 23 months to reach $2 billion. Global commerce snowballs.

The most recent global Fortune 500 list includes 35 Chinese firms; 3 from Hong Kong and 6 from Taiwan. The country's largest oil refiner Sinopec led the Chinese group at 16th place, followed by State Grid, ranking at 24th, China National Petroleum at 25th, Hon Hai Precision Industry at 132nd, and ICBC at 133rd. The list also included 19 state-owned Chinese companies as well as China's top banks including the Industrial and Commercial Bank of China, China Construction Bank, Bank of China, and Agricultural Bank of China.

The global Fortune 500 list was topped by U.S. retailer Wal-Mart with sales of US$378.8 billion followed by Exxon Mobil with sales of US$372.8 billion, Royal Dutch Shell with US$355.7 billion, BP with US$291.4 billion, and Toyota Motor with US$230.2 billion. American companies occupied 153 places among the top 500—9 companies fewer than the previous year's 162. The list featured 64 Japanese firms, 39 French firms, 37 German firms, and 34 British firms. India had seven companies in the list led by Indian Oil and Reliance Industries; while Russia had five, including its biggest oil company, Gazprom.[2]

Imagine if we had posited this cosmopolitan corporate mix 20 years ago. Chinese corporate giants! A retailer top of the U.S. corporate tree! It was unimaginable.

Let's be clear: globalization has been a force for good, but as it stands, is far from perfect. An enormous divide remains between the haves and have-nots. While developed economies grow more prosperous over time, hundreds of millions of people remain untouched by the benefits of globalization.

Take global poverty, for example, defined by the World Bank as living on less than $1.25 a day. According to 2008 World Bank figures 1.4 billion people (one in four) in the developing world were living on less than $1.25 a day in 2005. The global picture is one of widely varying experiences. While living standards have improved dramatically in some regions—poverty in East Asia has fallen from approximately 80 percent of the population living on less than $1.25 a day in 1981 to 18 percent in 2005, for example—but in others there has been less progress—in absolute terms, the number of poor people has nearly doubled, from 200 million in 1981 to 380 million in 2005.[3]

And, as we have learned, recessions can now also go global. Globalization comes with a price. But, sort this out, and the prize makes it worthwhile—and people respect you for it.

Multinationals lead the way

Multinational corporations and those who lead them are at the forefront of globalization. Multinational corporations are the great organizations of our times. Around the world, cityscapes are distinguished by glass-fronted corporate cathedrals rather than their stain-glassed religious predecessors. "Corporations are the dominant social institutions of our age," says Richard Pascale. Multinationals have shaped the way globalization has happened and now impacts on our lives.

Armed with border-breaking technology, modern-day multinationals have exploited the opportunities created by globalization with a steady stream of foreign alliances and mergers and acquisitions among regions and industries. The urge for many remains fundamentally imperialist. They want to conquer the world and, for those they encounter, it sometimes feels like the invasion of an imperialist army.

For those aware of corporate history this does not really come as a surprise. Corporations have traditionally been more adventurous than we often think. Consider the globalizing exploits of the East India Company four hundred years ago or the Hudson Bay Company in the Americas, for instance.

The English East India Company is a good example of the Imperialist approach to extending activities into other cultures. Founded in 1600 to trade in the East Indies, it was not long before the Company was firmly established in India. It swiftly colonized large swathes of India, raising armies, fighting battles, and imposing rule through direct governance and feudal alliances, in a period known as the Company Raj. It wasn't until much later in the 1800s that the East India Company's territories were brought under the governance of the UK government.

Understandably there was considerable resentment among the indigenous population. There were various uprisings most notably the Indian Rebellion of 1857, which began as a mutiny against the British East India Company's army, and spread rapidly threatening the Company's power in the region. The uprising is also known as India's First War of Independence.

Contrast the East India Company's approach with that of the French government's approach to trading in Canada. While it had a monopoly on the Canadian fur trade in the seventeenth century, the French government preferred to establish trading posts in the interior of what is the drainage bay of the Hudson River and adjoining lands, have traders live with local tribes, and encourage farming activities rather than outright exploitation of the local population.

Not so with the British. They backed two French entrepreneurs in a trading endeavor under the auspices of a Royal Charter from Charles II. The Governor and Company of Adventurers of England trading into Hudson's Bay, founded in 1670, built a series of trading forts adopting a far less integrated more confrontational approach. Interestingly the company survives to this day, albeit with a shorter name, and is one of the oldest companies in the world.

In their more modern incarnation, multinationals have been a globalizing force. Both supply chains and markets are global as never before. But, the typical corporate globalization model remains stubbornly colonial in its ambition and execution. The world is colonized one market at a time. In the past, colonial behavior in distant foreign outposts was accepted. Companies preserved their cultures and ways of doing things no matter what the local culture. Expatriate managers patiently explained how things were done to keen-to-learn locals.

As Stuart Crainer and Des Dearlove, visiting professors at IE Business School in Madrid, have observed: "In the early 1980s, the Harvard marketing guru Ted Levitt implored companies to think global; act local. Today, the challenge is to act global; think local. But that is easier said than done. Most companies content themselves with the easier axiom of: talk global; and act like you do at home."[4]

German misadventures[5]

Consider what happened when Wal-Mart moved into Germany. The retailer entered Germany in 1997, and grew its presence to 85 stores. Then in 2006, in a remarkable volte-face it sold the lot to Metro. Along the way from launch to sell-off, Wal-Mart's problems were many and varied.

Wal-Mart's corporate culture rests on a particular way of doing business, focused ruthlessly on efficiency in all aspects—supplier relations, store locations, and human resources. In addition, the company prides itself on operating from Bentonville, Arkansas, far away from Washington and the world of politics. It tried to keep a very low profile. This model, and the deliberately apolitical management style, clashed with German expectations about how a company should be run. The Wal-Mart ethics code appeared draconian to German eyes and caused a media furor—it was interpreted as being down on relationships between employees and encouraging of people telling tales on their colleagues. Putting groceries in bags for customers also went down badly as Germans prefer to handle their own groceries. Add in intense local competition and a preference for local food and products, and Germany proved an expensive misadventure for Wal-Mart—the estimated cost to the company was $1 billion.

It is not as if Wal-Mart is a stranger to expansion. It opened a Supercenter and a Sam's Club in Shenzhen, China in 1996, well before China became the economic flavor of the month. But it suggests that conquering the world is not as easy as it sometimes looks from the comfort of corporate HQ.

Large American corporations have encountered similar difficulties to those experienced by Wal-Mart in Germany though it should be noted that the perils of global growth are not solely an American preserve.

The online auctioneer eBay misfired in China in the face of local competition from Alibaba among others. The all-American company, Amway, has similarly enjoyed mixed fortunes. It entered the Chinese market in 1995 and quickly expanded. Then Amway was banned from China, in April 1998, after a government clampdown on direct marketing. Amway's pyramid selling model was worryingly direct and successful; a mass movement which unsettled the Chinese government suspicious of what it called "evil cults, secret societies and superstitious and lawless activities" (*sic*). Three months later, Amway was allowed to operate once again selling through retail outlets. It won back a direct sales license in 2006 and is now thriving.

Today, the more enlightened companies do not take an imperialist approach. Instead, they demonstrate sensitivity and attempt to integrate corporation and community. They have realized that pitting company against company—whether they are producers or distributors—is no longer a viable competitive option to gain market share. In a dog-eat-dog world, you eventually run out of dogs. At its best, global competition is now more focused on improving product and service quality and reducing costs through innovation and technological advances.

Diminishing nation states

The forces of globalization are taking economic development beyond the control of nation states. For better or worse, international financial institutions and multinational companies now play the major role in shaping decisions on trade, economies, and development. Consider what happened to Iceland in the face of financial turmoil: a nation was rendered bankrupt. Without a big enough skilled workforce, developing countries struggle to govern global organizations. Only the great superpowers can still hold sway over the burgeoning power of corporations.

For example, as we were writing this book, America exerted its economic might over the Swiss bank UBS by insisting it disclose a confidential list of its clients. In February 2009, UBS handed over the names of approximately 300 customers. It avoided criminal charges in the United States where it earns more money than in its domestic market. In the next month, UBS lost 22 percent of its market value.[6] Imagine you were a UBS executive charged with making such politically, culturally, and commercially loaded decisions.

The sight of superpowers flexing their muscles over corporations is increasingly rare. Nationalism was a building block in establishing individual states. Now, the ideology of nationalism, emphasizing the individual culture, formative context, history and language of each nation, is being challenged by the new international system of trade. This, in turn, erodes the uniqueness of national identities by increasing migration and understanding of other communication patterns and national cultures. Simultaneously, new global governance standards and institutions, as well as the continual opening of markets, further erodes the power of the individual state.

"The nation state promised much, but delivered little. In today's world, far from making things better it threatens to make them worse. It has the potential to hold back human development through artificial compartmentalization of skills and markets. Quite simply, the world has moved on," argues the Japanese thinker Kenichi Ohmae in his book, *The Next Global Stage*. "Our world is now interdependent to a greater degree than ever before. But global interdependence is *nothing* new. The idea of a hermetically sealed nation state fully self-sufficient in all its needs is absurd. There has always been trade. Throughout human history technology has made trade possible over greater distances. Now, technology and improved logistics allow trade to occur at greater speed.

Nation states, by breaking up the world's population into supposedly self-sufficient entities have stymied the realization of interdependence."[7]

One clear side effect of the diminishing power of nation states—and one which Kenichi Ohmae has tracked over the past decade—is the growing importance of regions. Increasingly, business leaders will have to understand the dynamics, politics, and personalities of different regions rather than nations.

New forces at work

With globalization come greater responsibilities and influence. With power comes responsibility. This is already being exercised—and in different arenas than national parliaments and boardrooms. Think of the World Economic Forum's annual meeting at the Swiss resort of Davos. It plays host to over 2,500 politicians, business leaders, and power brokers at the heart of the world's travails—and the most likely source of their solutions.

The World Economic Forum, a not-for-profit based organization, based in the small town of Coligny outside of Geneva in Switzerland, is the brainchild of German economist Klaus Schwab, formerly a professor at the University of Geneva.

Founded in 1971 by Schwab as the European Management Forum (it was renamed in 1987) the World Economic Forum is best known for the annual Davos meeting where some of the most powerful people in the world gather to further its mission of "improving the state of the world." Davos is not the only event held under the auspices of the World Economic Forum, however. Regional gatherings are held around the world on an annual basis.

Critics say that the World Economic Forum is a convenient venue for executives from the most powerful companies to broker deals behind closed doors and set the agenda, while indulging in a little skiing. The World Economic Forum counters that! Increasingly decisions about the future of business and society need to involve all stakeholders. Davos and the other regional meetings bring those stakeholders together and encourage dialog and debate between them.

Either way, the influence of the World Economic Forum at Davos on global economic and business decision-making shows no signs of receding.

The 2009 Davos meeting was undoubtedly the most technologically advanced. This helped bring the debate to a much greater audience than ever before. For the first time, the social networking platform Facebook ran real-time polls of its 150 million users. Over 120,000 people responded to a single poll on the stimulus package to get economies out of the crisis. The Davos debates on YouTube have been watched over 2.7 million times.

All of this is a long way from the more humble roots of the annual meeting. Davos widens the debate but it is a debate with corporate CEOs at its heart. Similar changes can be seen at other global forums such as G8, the Trilateral Commission, and even the Bilderberg Group—viewed as a slightly mysterious group, founded in the 1950s, which draws together a small number of powerful people annually at various locations around the world, in Athens in 2009 for example, and is notable for being the subject of numerous conspiracy theories—where business leaders largely set the agenda. In reality, Bilderberg's influence is profoundly positive, determining ways of thinking for the future among elites on a global scale.

We shouldn't really be surprised by such organizations. Politics and business are long-term bedfellows. How do you get access to the prime ministers office? That's something that is a requirement if you want deals in parts of Africa.

Increasingly, multinationals find themselves dealing with what have been labeled nonmarket forces. Among those leading the way in studying nonmarket forces is David Bach of Spain's IE Business School. "A firm not only maintains relationships with its customers, suppliers and competitors (what we can refer to collectively as the 'market environment') but also maintains relationships with governments, regulators, non-government organizations (NGOs), the media and society at large—whether it wants to or not. So, anyone can be affected by non-market forces and in very consequential ways," Bach explains.

One of the examples David Bach cites is Chiquita Brands. In the 1990s the company sourced most of its bananas from Latin America and Europe was its biggest market. Meanwhile, the European Union was changing its banana policies to favor non-Latin American suppliers. Chiquita completely missed this non-market event and suffered as a result. Its banana rival Dole, on the other hand, was tracking the workings of the Commission, diversified its suppliers and succeeded in improving its business as a result.

"When I think of examples like this, I often recall the phrase that captures the danger of not being engaged in political processes central to your business: 'If you're not at the table, you're on the menu'," says Bach. Non-market forces have always been a part of the business world, and some companies have been somewhat cognizant of their importance. But, in the main, companies have not given these matters much thought. They took the non-market environment for granted, as something that was given. It wasn't seen as part of the playing field. Think about all the strategic plans that have been developed in the last two decades. How many had a section on the company's nonmarket strategy? Our guess? Not many. Most, by far, did not focus in any serious way on this aspect of their competitive position. We believe the error here is a matter of emphasis.

"Firms ought to apply the same rigour to the formulation and implementation of non-market strategy as they do to the formulation and implementation of their regular market strategy. But this alone is insufficient. Firms then must integrate market and non-market strategies to make sure they are consistent and coherent. We are increasingly seeing that firms can create—or lose—competitive advantage in the non-market environment."[8]

All is not what it seems

As they navigate these nonmarket forces, multinationals have to put aside long-held assumptions. Instead of regarding governments as benign, good or bad, black or white, they need to appreciate the complex shades of gray which characterize modern governments.

Governments are multidimensional and while they may lay down the law they are as likely to adhere to chaotic lawlessness. Indeed, some of the greatest corruption is attributed to governments, and not the governments you would necessarily expect. Programs run for politicians, administrators, and senior managers from developing countries routinely identify that the U.S. and UK governments are far more corrupt than those of Russia and the Ukraine. The expenses scandal that engulfed British politics in 2009 suggests they have a point. The reason the story dominated the media for weeks, however, was because the British public had believed that their politicians were less corrupt than elsewhere. The corruption may be more sophisticated, discrete or civilized, but it is still there. What chance then does a corporation have when operating in these countries?

We were at a military training college in the United Kingdom when we heard members of the Nigerian army asking for advice from the British army concerning corruption in Nigeria instigated by Western oil companies. The Nigerians complained that though Western oil companies talked about corporate social responsibility, on the ground their behavior had antagonized local people so much that the army had been called in. The oil companies, according to our sources, "promptly put pressure on a number of governments, particularly the British and the U.S."

The growing responsibilities and influence of multinationals will bring them into many more situations where the boundaries between government and commerce are, at best, fuzzy and, at worst, unworkable.

Paradox central

So, globalization rules and is reshaping the rules of life, government, and business. There is no longer anything particularly contentious with this statement. Globalization is a fact of life.

But—and it is a large and significant *but*—as the world has seemed to become more homogenous, our differences have actually become more important than ever. This is the paradox at the heart of globalization: As business has become more global the need to be more sensitive to local nuances has increased.

The nature of the challenge for organizations and those who lead them has changed over recent years. Once the overriding emphasis was on global expansion. Now, having conquered the world (at least by their old measures) global corporations are often challenged by the emergence of differences in national systems, and internal governance systems. Their new emphasis must be on fostering relationships between individuals and business units. They are no longer concerned with external conquest and more concerned with internal fighting. The office in London often competes with its counterpart in Frankfurt or New York. They need alignment and minimal friction to continue to be competitive. And, as we shall now see, they have to achieve these things in an often bewilderingly complex world.

Ask Yourself

- How has globalization affected you and your organization?
- How will it affect you and your organization in the future?
- How do you ensure you are sensitive to local nuances?
- How do you ensure the same is true of your colleagues?
- How do you ensure your organization is local and global?
- How do you manage and shape nonmarket forces?

Be comfortable with complexity

As the world shifts from homogeneity to heterogeneity, complexity lurks at every corner. Learn to love it. Fortune favors the inquiring mind.

The complex world

As the business world has globalized, the level of complexity that business leaders and many others encounter in their daily working lives has increased massively. Thanks to travel and technology, problems are never solely local in their ramifications and potential solutions. Everything and, increasingly, everyone connects. Complexity is no longer a theoretical case of a butterfly fluttering its wings in an Amazonian rainforest, but of someone picking up their BlackBerry in Vietnam and making a request of their colleague in Sweden. It happens every day.

Techno-visionaries Vernor Vinge and Ray Kurzweil confidently forecast that within just 20 years the problem-solving and policy-making environment will have become so complex that we will have to embed computerized thinking aides in our brains, simply to make informed, intelligent decisions.

In his book *The Singularity Is Near, When Humans Transcend Biology*, Kurzweil presents a vision of the future where, in the fifth human epoch, biology and computers will merge. Computers will be smarter than humans. (What's the betting we will still be shouting at them though, when they suddenly shut down for no apparent reason?)

Kurzweil describes the approaching Singularity thus: "... a future period during which the pace of technological change will be so rapid, its impact so deep, that human life will be irreversibly transformed. Although neither utopian nor dystopian, this epoch will transform the concepts that we rely on to give meaning to our lives, from our business models to the cycle of human life, including death itself."[9]

Of course, complexity has been discussed in a myriad of different phrases and from a profusion of perspectives for decades. Back in 1970 the British cyberneticist Stafford Beer testified before the U.S. Congress and argued that the overarching challenge of our age was going to be "managing modern complexity." Needing to do more of whatever one is doing has become an apparently habitual urge of our time. Multitasking is a constant reality—just watch any young person listening to their iPod while composing a text message, logging onto Facebook while casting an occasional glance at the TV screen. The challenge of managing beyond modern complexity is enormous and has spawned the term "complexipacity."[10]

Complexipacity embraces the new realities of social life. This is characterized by the complexity and indefiniteness of the social environment; the fragmentation and specialization of knowledge; increasingly having to deal with aims that conflict with each other; and a multiple process of decision-making.

Of course, some skeptics dismiss the complexity challenge as more apparent than real or, at best, a transitory phenomenon that will quickly be subsumed by automated systems for monitoring and applying routine decision information.

They may be right, but even if we delegate important institutional and individual choices to "intelligent systems," can we really abdicate our responsibility for understanding how those systems work and what they actually do? Or will we turn that responsibility over to intelligent systems as well, endowing them with the complexipacity we cannot achieve?

Whatever happens, it is increasingly clear that growing complexity in our day-to-day decisions demands an entirely new set of basic skills.

A to B

To better understand what these new skills might be, it is worth considering the traditional thinking which has dominated organizational life over much of the past century—if not longer. Traditional thinking is static. It takes a point in time, focuses on particular events and causes and effects. It tends to be linear and views behavior as driven by external forces. It is built on the belief that really knowing something means focusing on the details and this leads to its fundamental faith in the usefulness of measurement. The search for perfectly measured data can be seen in organizations throughout the world, where data often dominate to the point of standing in the way of—and sometimes destroying—creativity and innovation.

Complexipacity demands a more holistic approach, one that embraces systemic thinking, collaborative collegiality, problem-solving, continuous learning, and creativity, among other things.

Holistic thinking involves a combination of at least three types of thinking.[11]

Dynamic thinking

- Framing a problem in terms of a pattern of behavior over time
- System-as-cause thinking
- Placing responsibility for a behavior on internal actors who manage the policies and plumbing of the system
- Forest rather than tree-to-tree thinking
- Believing that, to know something, one must understand the context of relationships

Operational thinking

- Concentrating on getting at causality and understanding how a behavior is actually generated
- Systems thinking

- Viewing causality as an ongoing process with the "effect" feeding back to influence the causes, and the causes affecting one another

Qualitative *and* quantitative thinking

- Accepting that one can always quantify, but not always measure
- Scientific thinking—actively seeking out the facts and analysis which create the foundation for decision-making
- Recognizing that all models are working hypotheses that always have limited applicability

Complex implications

Clearly, dealing with complexity through holistic thinking has implications in a wide variety of areas both personal and organizational.

First, organizations are more complex than ever before. Ashby's law of requisite variety states that the complexity of an organization internally must match the complexity of its external environment.[12]

This has never been truer. It takes complexity to deal with complexity. If the market is complex you have to have inside complexity to deal with it.

At an operational level, corporations have to balance system restrictions and discretionary action. When it comes to the quality of delivery, the most common tensions are

- How to meet the needs of the local market?
- How to use discretion while bearing in mind cost issues, organizational protocols, and government issues?
- How to handle sensitive issues? These include, for example, the question of giving gifts not as a bribe but as tokens of friendship. This is frequently culturally necessary, but how do you get it through the expense system of a typical Western company?

- How does a manager adopt local values but still live the ethos of the corporation? Becoming *too* local is not always a good thing as it may mean losing authority, not being transparent, not encouraging diversity, and so on.
- How does a manager implement certain global strategies concerning branding, marketing, and sales in a local context, which does not favorably respond to these strategies?
- How does a manager implement ethical practices in a local context that has different ethical concerns?
- How does the local manager handle the pricing of goods and services? This may necessitate offering concessions to favored customers, and renegotiating outsourcing relationships, which could make sense locally but go against corporate guidelines.
- How does a manager handle these tensions and yet develop trust with a local context and keep the trust of the corporation?
- In terms of organizational discipline, cost controls need to be balanced with flexible delivery. How can you emulate the flexible excellence of a retailer like Zara while keeping costs under control?

Complex Inc.

Given the burgeoning number of tensions and complications, new ways of approaching and resolving challenges have to be adopted and often innovated. A new locally attuned organizational model is emerging.

For example, to cut costs and understand customers, the better global corporations are integrating customers into their strategy and eliminating intermediaries.

The management thinker C. K. Prahalad has championed the concept of co-creation. "What it says is that we need two joint problem solvers, not a single problem solver," he explains. "In the traditional industrial system, the firm was the centre of the universe; but when you move to the new information age, consumers have the opportunity to engage in a dialogue and be active and, therefore, they can shape their own personal experiences. So, with co-creation, consumers can personalize their own experiences and the firm can benefit. And this is becoming much more common and possible today."[13]

Prahalad takes the example of Google. "If I look at Google, it does not tell me how to use the system; I can personalize my own page, I can create iGoogle. I decide what I want. Google is an experience platform. Google understands that it may have a hundred million consumers, but each one can do what they want with its platform. That is an extreme case of personalized, co-created value. Our shorthand for that is N=1."

"On the other hand, Google does not produce the content at all. The content comes from a large number of people around the world—institutions and individuals. Google aggregates it and makes it available to me. That is the spirit of co-creation, which says that even if you have a hundred million consumers, each consumer experience is different because it is co-created by that consumer and the organization, in this case Google. So resources are not contained within the firm, but accessed from a wide variety of institutions; therefore, resources are global. Our shorthand for that is R=G, because resources are now coming from more than one institution. So, N=1 and R=G are going to be the pattern for the future."

Simple visions for complex times

Why are we here and where are we going? The second challenge emphasized by complexity is that of providing a sense of purpose to any organization and to the individuals who make up the organization. In a global organization, local needs are often out of sync with global corporate goals.

From our Top Team research, we know that 33 percent of top teams are divided on the vision for the future of the organization. Inevitably this leads to a lot of infighting. Also 66 percent of top teams find it very difficult to raise this uncomfortable fact. Little wonder that negative and untrustworthy cultures abound.

There are—sometimes glorious—exceptions. The Tata Group, the second biggest company in India, comprises of over 100 different companies and subsidiaries, including Tata Motors, Tata Steel, Corus Steel, Tata Consultancy Services, Tata Technologies, Tata Tea, and the Taj Hotels, operating in over 80 countries.

Yet if you visit Tata, led by its renowned chief executive and chairman, Ratan Tata, you will quickly realize that his talent lies in taking a bewildering portfolio of products, positioning them differently in different parts of the world, and still having an overriding philosophy.

Tata has ensured that the unique character and culture of the Tata Group, one of the most progressive companies in India, is preserved as it expands across the globe, maintaining the spirit of a company that introduced the eight-hour working day, maternity leave, and profit-sharing for employees, well before many of its Western counterparts.

Tata has realized that to succeed there has to be some degree of shared understanding of the world out there today and in the future. There has to be what Sir Colin Chandler, former chairman of budget airline easyJet, calls, "A common understanding of what the business is about."[14]

Providing a shared sense of what the organization stands for and where the organization would like to be is a key discipline of global leaders. They help people in the organization make sense of the present and the future so that they and the organization can maximize their performance now and in the future.

This is about helping others to make sense of past and present processes and events, so that a shared understanding of the strategy, vision, and mission of the enterprise emerges for both the board and management. Shared understanding acts as a primary platform for action; the confidence that the leadership of the organization are of one mind. Visibly evident shared commitment at the level of the top team bonds together everyone else in the organization.

This begins with some key business questions:

- What is the competitive advantage of the firm?
- Do customers recognize the value this firm provides?
- Is the reality that most customers can barely tell the difference

between one company's services except for those at the very top of the value chain?

- Is price the only real differentiator from the customer's point of view?
- What do shareholders expect in terms of return on their investment?
- Is greater value to be gained from keeping the enterprise together or separating out the assets for sale?

Would the people in your organization answer these questions on the same foundation of knowledge and aspiration? Word-for-word, learned by rote answers aren't what is needed. People need to sing from the same hymn sheet—and at the very least, know that such a sheet is available (hopefully from the CEO's office).

Dos and don'ts

Companies can never stand still. There is constant tension between the need for integration—to be tightly and profitably managed—and capital growth.

Figuring out what you do and don't do is increasingly problematic. It used to be straightforward to establish the boundaries of what an organization did and didn't do. This is no longer true. To beat complexity—or at least to stay at the same pace—companies must figure out what and where their key operations are.

Companies once existed without answering some basic questions. Their sense of what was core, critical, and nice to have for their business was barely acknowledged in the strategic debate. No longer. Now, these three issues should be a distinct part of the debate. The trouble is that our research has found that they are not.

That they should be is borne out by the work of John Browne at BP. Browne, we have been told by BP executives, was able to reconceptualize BP in a way that fundamentally redirected resources. The outsourcing of BP's exploration activities challenged one of the sacred cows of the business—that it was primarily an exploration-led company. It was a statement that the company's focus was now on transportation and logistics.

Browne's willingness to challenge the status quo was a vital part of his success. He asked the unaskable and challenged the unchallengeable. Viewed as highly rational and seemingly with little sensitivity to local customs, the three big questions Browne posed were

- What is the essence/purpose of the BP brand in the future?
- What is BP's competitive advantage/differentiator?
- How do the directors add value?

How many other leaders have the confidence to ask such fundamental questions? In our experience, very few. Yet to leverage complexity they are crucial.

Vodka with everything

The popular version of the success of the Smirnoff vodka brand story recounts how the design consultants, a New York firm, came up with the clear bottle design, with, at the other end of the clear bottle, an image of beauty, often female but clad in such a way that, that beauty made sense in that local country or context. Drink Smirnoff the campaign suggested and maybe you too can acquire the beauty you see through the bottle.

And this is all true. The reality of Smirnoff's success, however, is a little more prosaic and in large part down to the hard work, determination, and cultural sensitivities of its CEO at the time, a Tanzanian-born, Greek executive, Dennis Malamatinas.

At the time IDV, the company that owned Smirnoff, was structured as three single brand companies: Smirnoff vodka, Baileys Irish cream, and a whisky company, plus a number of regional and local country companies. The intention was for Smirnoff to become a global brand and in order to do that Smirnoff required global reach and spread.

The problem was that Smirnoff was popular in certain parts of the world but not in others. In Germany, for example, Smirnoff was some way down the list of most favorite tipples in IDV's stable of drinks, and so it needed the head of the German operation to promote the vodka brand, and move it a little higher up the list of drinks consumed.

Unfortunately for Malamatinas, the head of Germany reported to the head of Europe, who determined the marketing budget for the Germany company manager. And it was a similar position in a number of other countries. Smirnoff faced a classic obstacle to its global success—regional priorities were not aligned with the global brand strategy. In fact, country managers who promoted Smirnoff were in danger of missing their own targets for other brands. There were conflicting priorities. In our experience these sorts of tensions between local and global operations are commonplace. What to do?

Malamatinas identified the countries that needed an additional push to promote Smirnoff, and met with each of the relevant country managers and tried to get them to promote Smirnoff on the basis of a personal understanding and relationship.

In addition, realizing that the country managers were at risk of being reprimanded by their senior regional managers if they spent too much of their marketing budget on Smirnoff, Malamatinas agreed to take the blame and resign if any of the managers came under pressure and were dismissed.

He also made sure that he championed the country managers with the regional directors he dealt with as part of IDV's senior management team.

Malamatinas and a small team spent approximately 12 months or so running around the world forming links with the country managers he had identified, convincing them that Smirnoff should be placed higher on their list of priorities, even though it was not a popular local drink.

The net result was that Smirnoff increased its sales in a period of about ten months from approximately 11 million cases a year to approximately 20 million cases a year. A global brand was born, but only because Malamatinas understood—and neutralized—the conflicting pressures within his own company. That is the reality of global leadership.

The art of outsourcing

In the modern business world, such conflicts of interest abound. Look at outsourcing. What is outsourcing? It is taking a resource that somebody else can handle on your behalf, better than you could yourself. That suggests its dynamic. What you sourced out today you might want to take back in tomorrow. Or next year. So you can't even talk about outsourcing globally now, you can only talk about sourcing. Yet, for all its economic rationale, outsourcing is rarely based on pure efficiency. There is usually a large dose of politics involved. Often the politics are internal—rooted in the cultural beliefs of the organization. At BP, for example, the cultural assumptions made exploration difficult to outsource, until John Browne brought a detached point of view.

Companies often don't outsource what's nice to have. In 2000 NatWest was taken over by Royal Bank of Scotland. In that year NatWest became the very first UK bank to make £2 billion profit. So, why did the shareholders decide that they would sell the United Kingdom's most profitable bank to Royal Bank of Scotland? What the shareholders saw was that the management of NatWest would not let go of its cultural legacy. The bank was already highly profitable despite hanging onto an old-fashioned view of its assets. The shareholders figured if the bank had somebody else managing its resources they would make even more profit.

One of NatWest's big problems, its managers have told us, was the location of its premises, and particularly its headquarters in the city of London. The company's leaders were culturally attached to it. This led to poor decisions. A former NatWest chairman took the whole of the ground floor of NatWest headquarters and turned it into an art gallery. This appears to have been the chairman's personal hobbyhorse. In truth, there was a strategic logic, a desire to position the bank as interested in the arts, as a sophisticated global brand, excelling at modern finance but also a vibrant part of the community. Unfortunately, the positioning was not clearly articulated or thought through. Anybody from the street could go into the art gallery. But NatWest employees were asked to stay out. The effect was to alienate employees from the organization and to make them feel unvalued.

So, although there was a strategic logic to the decision it misfired. If the chairman's aim was to address the bank's possession of an extremely valuable piece of real estate in the center of London and create a public service from it, then it was a laudable intention. In that case it was meant to say to shareholders and other stakeholders, we may be in the financial services business but look how sophisticated we are. Did it make any difference to the business? No. The managers we spoke to said it damaged morale. The decision to turn it into an art gallery actually made the business worse. Staff and shareholders asked why are you spending shareholder funds doing this? Why are we using the property this way? A sophisticated brand building initiative became an embarrassing diversion. Perhaps, the chairman identified his own cultural passions for the arts too closely with the best interests of the bank.

The internal governance of multinationals is an area of growing tension. They need to change the way they think and act both locally and regionally. They need to understand opportunities and risks. Where should they open a manufacturing plant? And where should they close one?

In a dynamic and highly competitive environment, many leaders and managers may disagree about which direction to take or what the corporate vision should be. Indeed, such decisions are often about balancing conflicting local/global agendas. These differences of opinion can further challenge the internal governance. The initiatives of influence, compromise, negotiation, and consensus building are crucial, especially when business transcends language and culture across the globe. Internal governance also needs to address the different forms of alliances a multinational corporation can enter into globally to ensure entrance into certain markets, including new standards and technologies required by the continuing growth of globalization.[15]

Successful global companies are ones that are capable of under-standing global logistics, have a flexible supplier base, are capable of addressing local environmental and social issues and understand the culture where they are established or seeking to expand into. They have been described as *ambidextrous*, in that they are capable of behaving and viewing the world in different ways at different times. Difference rules.

The complex organization

We have identified four tension points that affect global corporations.

Four tensions of the global corporation

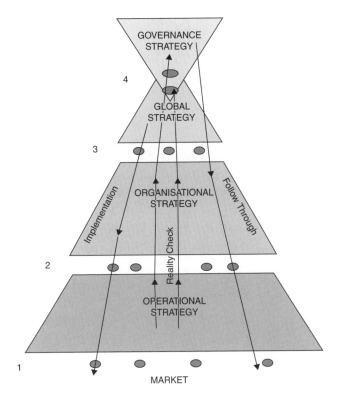

Tension Points

4- **Stewardship**–governance audits vs. leadership discretionary action

3- **Corporate Growth**–corporate integration vs. capital growth

2- **Organisation Discipline**–Cost controls vs. delivery flexibility

1- **Quality of Delivery**–system restrictions vs. customer service

Negotiate through these tension points and make that all embracing difference, now that's the hallmark of the global executive.

Ask Yourself

- What are the underlying tensions in your organization?
- Are employees pulled in different directions at the same time? If so, why?
- What are the paradoxes built into your strategy?
- Are these tensions and paradoxes resolvable—or is it a case of managing your way through them?
- Are the managers in your organization stressed—or do they realize that these tensions are normal?

Redefine leadership

To lead in the global arena, you must begin by rethinking every-thing you know and assume about leadership.

The need for leaders

In this global and complex business world, leadership is critical. Thriving in the global marketplace demands leadership. Yet, time and time again, we have witnessed companies make significant cultural and commercial blunders thanks to indifferent and insensitive leadership.

We worked with an Australian finance company that bought a subsidiary in the United Kingdom. The sales operation of the UK company was built on local informal networks. The Australian company insisted on its own approach to sales and spent millions on retraining. Despite the new shared language, it managed to totally misread the local culture and the strengths of the subsidiary. Competitive advantage and differentiation were simply not translated to the local context. The UK firm's business model was built upon a part-time sales force where the sales team lived within the communities they served. But this did not fit with the way the Australian parent company wanted to operate so it tried to impose its structure on the newly acquired firm. The result was a total mismatch of cultures and business models. Interestingly, too, the Australian management actually understood what the problem was—but they simply chose to ignore it, assuming that they could bulldoze the British customers into doing business their way. As a consequence of this cultural insensitivity, they failed to achieve their strategic objectives. Once set on the wrong path, the Australians insisted on carrying on. Ego took over and losses mounted. The UK company eventually collapsed.

"Global CEOs need to be comfortable with people and comfortable with people from a range of cultures. The reality is that country specific cultures are still important and need to be borne in mind by all business leaders," says Kevin Kelly, the American-born CEO of Heidrick & Struggles in his book *CEO*. "I realized early on when I came to Europe that my leadership approach would need to change. Americans, and to some extent, Asian countries generally enjoy a far more directive management approach. They expect the leader to lead. In Europe, I could not dictate and direct what I wanted to do (if I wanted anyone to actually do it). Instead I needed to consult and then discuss and listen to the thoughts of others. Even if I didn't use the suggestions given to me the Europeans needed to be consulted. This did mean decisions took longer to make but in the long run it was worth it, and enabled me to gain the trust and loyalty of my European colleagues."[16]

Kelly goes on to cite the example of a U.S. CEO who was appointed to run a bank in Asia. He got there and told everyone what they were doing was basically wrong, not the way it needed to be done. He lasted six months because, though he could run a U.S.-based global bank, an Asia-based global bank offered an entirely different set of cultural challenges.

There are a myriad of other such examples. Leaders screw up. We were in Australia recently when a telecoms company was thrown out of the bidding process for a national broadband network after its bid failed to conform. This mistake led to a dramatic collapse in the company's market value. And yet we have never encountered a leader who didn't want to get things right. Leaders try their damnedest and still sometimes get it wrong. Why? Because our expectations of leaders are enormous.

We expect Renaissance men and women to lead our organizations. Instead, we find mere mortals.

"The fact is that executive life has changed. Only 20 years ago, the capabilities required of successful executives were functionally-oriented. Apart from occasional forays to overseas subsidiaries, executive life was mono-cultural. The role of senior executives was carefully—perhaps comfortably—delineated. Communication was local, personal, and managed to fit the executive's convenience. Markets were monolithic, and reassuringly stable," say Laura Tyson, former dean of London Business School, and former GE executive Nigel Andrews, who led a research project into the emerging training requirements of organizations based on more than 100 face-to-face interviews with executives from global companies across a variety of industries and geographies. "Globalization is not simply about the transfer of work to emerging economies. Globalization is an art—an art of human relations which, like other arts, is premised on insights gleaned from teaching and from experience, and honed by continual practice, day in and day out, in the executive suites of the world's corporations. Globalization is about the exercise of management and leadership, on a worldwide scale."[17]

The research at London Business School concluded that companies require executives with what they label, *global business capabilities*—"the power to think, decide and act efficiently and innovatively in an unpredictable global business environment."

In their book *A Future Perfect: The Challenge and Hidden Promise of Globalization*, the *Economist's* John Micklethwait and Adrian Wooldridge, coined the term *cosmocrat*—a contraction of cosmopolitan and bureaucrat—meaning a cosmopolitan businessperson and member of an emerging imagined global ruling elite.

"We talk of the rise of a class of cosmocrats—perhaps 20 million people worldwide. This class is in the process of forming," Micklethwait and Wooldridge explained. "It is made up of people who have similar global lifestyles and who possess the ideas, connections, and sheer chutzpah to master the international economy. It is a formally meritocratic class produced by Western education systems and companies. Yet, while there is a great feeling among Western educated people that their values are universal, their institutions are not very good at reaching out to the developing world. Western educational institutions and companies should be reaching out to recruit the talented people from developing countries."[18]

Micklethwait and Wooldridge envisaged that the number of cosmocrats would approximately double by 2010 and anticipated that China, India, and Brazil would begin producing their own cosmocrats. They have. India, in particular, has created a spectacularly large leadership production line. Even so, it is not enough: simply, there are not enough global leaders to go round.

Cosmo man and woman

It is worth bearing in mind that notions of "world citizenship" and cosmopolitanism have been discussed for centuries. It was Socrates, Aristotle, as well as the Stoics such as Diogenes and Zeno, who proclaimed themselves to be "citizens of the world."

In the modern era, Immanuel Kant furthered the cosmopolitan agenda. Kant argued that "since the narrower or wider community of the people of the earth has developed so far that a violation of rights in one place is felt throughout the world, the idea of a law of world citizenship is no high-flown or exaggerated notion." Given that he was writing in the eighteenth century, the prescience of his words is astounding. Kant's work led to three principles of cosmopolitanism—individualism, universality, and generality.

We believe that cosmopolitanism has never been more relevant. It encourages broad political latitude for the expression of varied values and ideologies in a rapidly evolving local and global environment. Cosmopolitanism is locally grounded while being world-oriented.

Make no mistake, leadership on the global stage is often impossibly demanding. Many leaders and managers find it challenging to operate and work in the multiple environments they are involved in. The challenges come from rapid and significant changes occurring in societies—such as societal behaviors toward innovation and change; changes in authority; and new roles for leaders as change agents rather than administrators.

Confusing leadership

Many leaders we encounter tackle these challenges simply by doing more. They rack up 100,000 miles and flying points every year. They spend hours on long-distance calls and emails. They live in hotel rooms rather than at home. (Indeed, the executive coach Ram Charan travels so much that until very recently he did not have a home and mailed his laundry back to his office in Dallas.) And all the time they are forging new relationships in new environments; losing contact with their cultural grounding and their community at home; adapting and developing entirely novel behavior in different multicultural settings; and forging relationships with companies, communities, and enemies. It is a continual managerial maelstrom, an assault to senses and emotions.

All of this means that staying in touch and maintaining relationships with loved ones becomes impossibly difficult. Families suffer and sometimes break down. Friendships are lost through neglect.

One executive we encountered was the relatively young chairman of companies in Europe and North America. He was a mathematician by training, but very sensitive to people. He found that long-distance calls and inter-flora didn't nurture long-term relationships. To change things he put himself in the position of everyone in his personal and professional network. When would they like to hear from him? What was going on in their lives that he should be concerned about? Having thought about his life and relationships in this way, the entire locus of his life changed. Yes, he still traveled, but when he did he ensured that he thought about other people and tried to manage his relationships.

Such groundedness is incredibly difficult to achieve. A unique approach to this is taken by the leadership coach Marshall Goldsmith who clocks up as many air miles as anyone we have encountered in our travels.

Every night, Goldsmith gets a phone call. It doesn't matter where he is in the world or how many hours he has worked that day: the phone still rings. On the other end of the line is Goldsmith's long-time friend and coach, Jim Moore. Every night, Moore asks him 13 questions.

The first question is always: "How happy are you?" Twelve others follow: "How much walking did you do? How many push-ups? How many sit-ups? Did you eat any high-fat foods? How much alcohol did you drink? How many hours of sleep did you get? How much time did you spend watching TV or surfing the Internet? How much time did you spend writing? Did you say or do something nice for your wife? Did you say or do something nice for your children? How many times did you try to prove you were right when it wasn't worth it? How many minutes did you spend on topics that didn't matter or that you can't control?"

Goldsmith calls them his baker's dozen. "They're the same questions each night," he explains, "and knowing Jim will call and that I have to answer them honestly is my method of following up on my goal of becoming a healthier individual."[19]

The trouble with leadership

One of the reasons why leaders travel so much and take on such punishing schedules is that it is an enormous job, but also one which is enormously open to interpretation. There is no job description for the CEO of a large global organization.

We asked a friend of ours who is a leader in the finance industry to explain how he saw his role. "First of all I think a global leader needs to take a long term view and not a short term one. I think a leader needs to be able to create out of a chaotic/difficult situation an opportunity for the organization as well as for every single employee. While things may be bad a global leader needs to have the gift not to further upset the people he may need desperately in the future to carry on being successful. There may not be money for paying a bonus (or not as much) but a good leader needs to find a way to communicate this intelligently (not through a note on the intranet) and be able to give something that makes one want to further give as much as one can. Through upsetting good people in bad times these people as soon as they have a chance will go and other good people won't join you as they are getting to know what has happened. Trust has been broken, so hard, that this is not going to be regained any time soon (or ever). I think the problem in such big organisations is that everyone has a boss above. No one actually takes responsibility for anything. A global leader needs to be able to gain trust from the market in order to be able to communicate the truth without creating panic rather than lying to satisfy people for a further ten days."

Such sentiments bear out our belief that leadership, as anybody knows who has actively sought to engage in it, is a complex social phenomenon lacking real boundaries and a clear definition. Indeed, there are hundreds of definitions of what constitutes leadership. The collection of behaviors, interactions, outcomes, and social phenomena labeled as leadership is heterogeneous and often contradictory, and complemented by a plethora of prescriptive advice on how to lead, guaranteed to justify almost any approach to leadership.

The reality is that no two global leaders are the same. This has led some observers, such as Chris Bartlett and the late Sumantra Ghoshal, to contend that "there is no such a thing as a universal global manager."[20] Rather they propose a model of management that balances local, regional, and global demands. They argue that global corporations need three kinds of managers—business managers, country managers, and functional managers—and a set of senior executives. All are or could be described as global managers. Where the business manager is the "strategist + architect + coordinator"; the country manager is the "sensor + builder + contributor"; the functional manager is the "scanner + cross-pollinator + champion"; and the senior executive is the "leader + talent scout + developer." Think back to the organizational tensions we highlighted earlier. Clearly, these also have an impact on the choices facing leaders.

And that's only the theory. In practice, leadership is an iceberg-like concept. The visible part is its style and process. The nature of this visible 10 percent is determined by the 90 percent invisible mass, rooted in religion, history, culture, politics, economy, technology, and so on.

East meets West

In different countries there are obvious differences in their leadership styles and processes. Even near neighbors, such as the United Kingdom and Germany, have very different attitudes and approaches to leadership.[21] Further afield, the 90 percent of the iceberg means that different approaches are more clearly different. (It is also worth remembering that there are as many differences *in* countries as between countries.)

One of the most intriguing differences in leadership is that between Eastern and Western attitudes and practices. As we have indicated, it is easy to fall into simplistic explanations of our similarities and our differences. But something that we have found helpful when thinking about the differences between Eastern and Western cultures is the notion of *orthodoxy* versus *orthopraxy*.

In the West, we tend to lean toward orthodoxy. In other words, we are concerned with what is the right thought or idea. This can make us sensitive to others telling us what we should think and to identifying dogma.

The Eastern way leans toward orthopraxy—or the practice of doing the right thing. Morality in Eastern cultures is often framed around: what is the correct behavior? Interestingly, Eastern cultures are often less concerned with what an individual thinks as long as their behavior conforms to the accepted social rules. They are less concerned with controlling what people think as long as they do what they are expected to do. You don't have to believe as long as you adhere to the norms of behavior.

This gives rise to different attitudes. In the West, we talk about "singing from the same hymn sheet." In other words, we have to have the same beliefs. But the equivalent idea in the East could be expressed as "singing in harmony with the choir." In Eastern cultures, it matters less what we believe as long as we are all acting together.

This explains why Japanese companies moving into the West have routinely encountered challenges to their approach.

Japanese car plants in the north east of England started off by telling the workers what to do. But, being told exactly what to do irritated the English workers. They could do the job, they said.

Simply the best

Yet even in the East substantial differences exist.

In *Best Leaders* the Taoist philosopher, Lao Tzu, observes

> Of the best leaders,
> People barely know that they exist;
> Next come those who are loved and praised;
> Next those who are held in awe;
> And lastly those who are despised.
> By not trusting people enough,
> We make them untrustworthy.
> Great leaders are silent workers:
> When their work is done,
> People say, 'We did it ourselves.'

True leaders, according to Lao Tzu, are "silent workers." They perform their assignment naturally and silently. They have the true power—the power that empowers others. They have the true ambition—the ambition that elevates others. They do so because they have understood that in the ultimate scheme of things, there are no "others." In their presence you feel that you can accomplish more. They benefit the world; they make it a better place to live, just by being in it. Their "self" is so inconspicuous that when the work is done and their mission accomplished, people say, "We did it ourselves."

The Chinese offer a different perspective on global leadership. It is founded on the inborn moral capacity for compassion (*ren*), a sense of rightness (*yi*), and reciprocity (*shu*).

Ren is a capacity for compassion or benevolence toward fellow humans. It is essentially expressed in social relationships. Interestingly, the Chinese word "*ren*" structurally is made up of the words "human" and "two."

Yi is basically a moral sense of rightness, a capacity to discern appropriateness and the right direction in acts and relationships. *Ren* and *yi* often work in unison to define morality and to guide actions.

Li represents the many etiquettes, norms, and protocols in both personal and institutional lives. The legitimacy of *li* is based on *ren* and *yi,* and only under this condition are people obliged to follow it. Though *li* by itself is not a virtue, observing *li* is a basic virtue.

Together, *ren-yi-li* form a moral core that spawns and sanctions an intricate web of behavior-guiding moral virtues. In addition, the virtues of wisdom and trustworthiness are equally important. Traditional Chinese culture and modern Chinese communities deem *ren*, *yi*, *li*, wisdom, and trustworthiness as the five cardinal virtues of humanity.

In addition, *Junzi*—a term coined by Confucius to describe his ideal human—is another crucial component of the moral system. *Junzi*, the exemplary Confucian moral person, possesses all the cardinal virtues espoused in Confucianism. As well as possessing the five cardinal virtues, *Junzi* also has other virtues and is ready and able to execute virtuous acts consistently. People, especially the intelligentsia and the ruling elites, are urged to emulate *Junzi* in thoughts and deeds, as their life-goal.

Confucianism regards a person as essentially social in nature. The nature of a person's self is defined and constituted by the bundles of his or her social relationships in the world. With his/her socially embedded self, a person's identity and place in the world are understood through his/her social attachments and positions in the social hierarchy. The implication of this conception is clear. Because of its socially embedded nature, a person's interests, goals, and well-being have to be socially shaped, nurtured, and constrained by the relationships the person is in. His or her social bonds are the sources of his/her indebtedness and the obligations that he/she should fulfill with respect to these relationships.

It is worth pointing out that the values of humanity, humility, and heterogeneity are also prominent in Buddhism, Hinduism, and other Eastern religions. In such religions the great leader knows when to lead from the front but also when to lead from the rear in order to develop up-and-coming leaders. Values such as maturity, resilience, and courage are balanced by warmth and being supportive in order to fully engage with internal and external stakeholders.

African ethics

Move further west and the ethical focus shifts. African ethics and morality are based on the veneration of ancestors, so the general character of African ethics, the central concern, is the management of life and maintenance of well-being within society. Individual ethical choices are made within the context of the community, that is, community in the inclusive sense. In such a context individual actions are evaluated and judged based on the effect that they have on the life of the community.

In particular, within the South African context, this view finds expression in the concept of *Ubuntu* and a similar notion is expressed in the Shona concept of *Ukama,* implying the relatedness between humans, environment, god, and ancestors. Simplified, the concept underpins the very communal nature of African society and by extension, its ethics.

The well-being of the individual and his or her interest are possible through the community where the community becomes a web of relationships.

This is well expressed in the Zulu saying, *umuntu ngumuntu ngabantu* (you are a person through others). In other words, the well-being of the individual and his/her interest is possible only through the community. As an ethical principle, *ubuntu* places a high value on sound human relations.

As a result, in traditional societies, no one was a stranger. Hospitality to strangers in the spirit of sharing was a respected value of the community.

Likewise, cruelty, murder, cheating, or stealing was sufficient to warrant ostracizing the individual through public censure.

Tradition demanded that those who have done shameful or immoral acts must be cleansed before they can be accepted back into the community. The community's history and life experience are the sources of African ethics. This source may vary and evolves from social customs, religious beliefs, regulations, social taboos, proverbs, and certain symbols. It places a high value on the role of the tribal chief, or leader—whose primary duty is to the community rather than the individual.

Cultural leadership

It is tempting to assume that such broader conceptions of leadership are increasingly embraced in the Anglo-American business world. But the reality is often different. In our experience, what is occurring is actually a hardening of the Anglo-American view of the world. This is disappointing. But there are some who are trying to swim against the tide.

For example, an increasing number of book titles combine spirituality and leadership. Perhaps the most Eastern-sounding and persuasive is Robert K. Greenleaf's *The Servant as Leader.* "The servant-leader is servant first," says Greenleaf. "It begins with the natural feeling that one wants to serve, to serve first. Then conscious choice brings one to aspire to lead. The difference manifests itself in the care taken by the servant-first to make sure that other people's highest priority needs are being served."[22]

The Greenleaf Center for Servant-Leadership describes servant-leadership as "a practical philosophy, which supports people who choose to serve first, and then lead as a way of expanding service to individuals and institutions. Servant-leaders may or may not hold formal leadership positions. Servant-leadership encourages collaboration, trust, foresight, listening, and the ethical use of power and empowerment."[23]

Larry C. Spears, CEO of the Greenleaf Center argues that there are ten characteristics of a servant-leader:

1. Listening:...deep commitment to listening intently to others...Listening also encompasses getting in touch with one's

own inner voice. Listening, coupled with periods of reflection, are essential to the growth and well-being of the servant-leader.

2. Empathy: The servant-leader strives to understand and empathize with others. People need to be accepted and recognized for their special and unique spirits.

3. Healing: The healing of relationships is a powerful force for transformation and integration. One of the great strengths of servant-leadership is the potential for healing one's self and one's relationship to others—servant-leaders recognize that they have an opportunity to help make whole those with whom they come in contact.

4. Awareness: General awareness, and especially self-awareness...helps one in understanding issues involving ethics, power and values. It lends itself to being able to view most situations from a more integrated, holistic position.

5. Persuasion: Another characteristic of servant-leaders is a reliance on persuasion, rather than on one's positional authority, in making decisions within an organization ... The servant-leader is effective at building consensus within groups.

6. Conceptualization: Servant-leaders seek to nurture their abilities to dream great dreams. The ability to look at a problem or an organization from a conceptualizing perspective means that one must think beyond day-to-day realities.

7. Foresight:...enables the servant-leader to understand the lessons from the past, the realities of the present, and the likely consequence of a decision for the future.

8. Stewardship: Peter Block (author of *Stewardship and The Empowered Manager*) has defined stewardship as "holding something in trust for another."...

9. Commitment to the growth of people: ... The servant-leader recognizes the tremendous responsibility to do everything in his or her power to nurture the personal and professional growth of employees and colleagues.

10. Building community: The servant-leader...seeks to identify some means for building community among those who work within a given institution.[24]

As the interest in such concepts as servant-leadership testifies, there is no insurmountable barrier between Western and Eastern leadership—if a leader is open enough to embrace difference. In fact, Western-style servant-leadership is found in Africa (Ubuntu, Harambee); East Asia (Daoist, Confucianism); the Mediterranean (Jewish); India (Hindu), and in the Arabias (Islam).

At the same time, leadership is a dynamic concept. One style might work in one Eastern area, while there is no guarantee that it will work in another Eastern area. So, a successful leadership style must be flexible. The style that individuals use will be based on a combination of their values, beliefs, and preferences, as well as the organizational cultural and norms which will encourage that style.

It is worth remembering, too, that leadership is also affected by economic circumstance. For example, Taiwan was severely influenced by the Asian Financial Crisis of the 1990s. Although it has a highly disciplined culture, its recent economic dynamism was originally built on a newfound entrepreneurial energy. This led to a host of small firms which, as they grew, embraced the cultural norms of discipline and strict adherence to rules. In combination these two behaviors helped the gradual development of larger business corporations. However, faced with the uncertainty caused by the Asian financial crisis many people in the country ceased to act entrepreneurially and reverted to more traditional cultural norms. Entrepreneurial flair diminished. People in Taiwan became prone to obeying rules from their superiors. This underlines how an underlying cultural tendency can be accentuated by a crisis.

In mainland China, the situation is quite different. Economic development has been accelerating fast and the labor market is very dynamic—people have more choices in their career path. Taking account of this situation, a rigid leadership style might curb individual motivation, and an open leadership style is likely to be preferable.

The global leadership challenge

So, what are the challenges faced by global leaders? Our own research suggests that global leaders have to wrestle with eight—sometimes paradoxical—challenges. They are

- perceptive *and* transformational
- reflective *and* visionary
- connected *and* distant
- focused *and* flexible
- humble *and* resilient
- collaborative *and* networked
- a catalyst *and* developer
- passionate *and* rational

Perceptive and transformational

The key thread in our findings is the ability of the individual to adapt to different cultures. The best global leaders we have met are culturally sensitive and perceptive, yet able to implement change on a much broader canvas. They are willing to explore the world and build relationships internally and externally. The ability to speak several languages is a considerable plus as is having been educated abroad. Global leadership is not a monolog but a conversation, a flexible process of mental meaning creation.

Global leaders delight in finding the unexpected in the familiar—and this starts with their own behavior. Their voyage of discovery is internal as well as external.

Their perceptiveness is driven by an appetite for change—they exhibit a willingness to transform behavior and performance. They interrogate what is going on—asking what messages they should take from economic, social, and political trends—in order to bring about change.

Reflective and visionary

It constantly surprises us that many of the most dynamic and successful global leaders with the most packed diaries seem to find the time to read extensively. Global leaders are often voracious readers. They are forever quoting something they have read.

Part of this is a reflective strain. They have the ability to take time out, at a slower pace, to notice the cultural lenses through which we habitually see. This provides them with alternative views of the company, its core competencies, the nature of leadership, and how to establish strategic priorities.

This may seem airy-fairy, but global leaders are often adept at switching from the big picture to the detail instantaneously. They need both. The person in front of them is the person the leader needs to connect with, but they must bring to this connection a sense of the bigger picture, what the organization is about. We were struck when we visited a Microsoft office in the United Kingdom by how much they were in tune with the language, outlook, and vision of their colleagues on the west coast of America. The language and consciousness of issues was the same.

Connected and distant

At the heart of senior-level decision-making is the combination of being fully engaged and connected with the data, the issues, and the people; while at the same time maintaining a sense of distance so that you can reach the best decision for the organization.

One CEO told us how the most startling and frightening moment of his career came soon after he became CEO. He had to decide whether to proceed with a multimillion pound IT program. It was a subject about which he knew nothing. He realized at that point that such decisions had to be made based on trust. Such trust can only come with the leader having strong connections throughout the organization and beyond.

Often this simply does not happen. CEOs are often out of touch. This is not a criticism of them. It is a function of human nature. Leaders are routinely insulated from the truth. The challenge for them is to maintain a constant connection with what is actually going on and what is on the minds of people. This does not happen accidentally. The best global leaders work really hard at keeping in touch and keeping lines of communication and information open at all times.

Focused and flexible

As an alternative perspective, think of the leader as an acrobat, handling multiple tasks in a rapidly changing business environment. The critical task for the leader is of walking the tightrope to balance stressful work commitments with a fulfilling personal life.

It is a difficult balancing act. The Canadian Henry Mintzberg was one of the first writers who debunked some of the myths surrounding the traditional managerial tasks by examining what leaders do on a day-to-day basis. Mintzberg found that they work on many different tasks at the same time. Their work is frequently interrupted, and does not fit neatly within the traditional managerial functions of planning, organizing, controlling, directing, and so forth. Leaders are constantly in the spotlight while dealing with multiple tasks, handling crises, managing time, and generally organizing their own work and the work of others. Sound familiar? If overwhelmed by such work situations, a leader inadvertently sends signals that could be detrimental to the morale of his or her people.

An effective leader has the ability to keep several balls in the air and is keenly aware of the differences between strategic, urgent, or immediate tasks with those that can easily be placed on the back burner. An effective leader is competent at identifying, setting, and communicating business priorities—especially during hectic and fast-changing times. This coordination is not always an easy task given the frequent interruptions, crises, meetings, and other "normal" work disruptions and distractions.

Humble and resilient

Within the Indian culture there is a sense of humility. On one occasion, we were late for a meeting at the Mumbai Stock Exchange. A room of 35 chairmen and chief executives, some of whom had a portfolio of 50 plus companies that they had to manage, was waiting. These were, not multimillionaires, but multibillionaires. We were late by over an hour because of a delayed flight and a laborious taxi journey from the airport. The audience sat there patiently. We expected them to be highly irritated—as we would have been. But their first reaction was sympathy for us—we must have been distressed being professional people, to have gone through all this, to know we were late, to keep them waiting. "We sat here and waited for you to make sure you did not feel distressed. We want you now to have a cup of tea, sit down, go for a walk, we'll wait another hour until you feel better," they said.

They meant it. This was a powerful lesson in humility and having concern for others. It can be traced easily back to Gandhi and his notion of the greater gain that one has through the giving of yourself. Unfortunately for so many, the opposite is true. Hedonism and power are dwarfed by the drive of CEOs and chairmen to establish their legacies. Ego is everyone's worst enemy.[25]

The need for humility and resilience links to the notion of the authentic leader. Understanding and being true to yourself lie at the heart of being confident, a contentment with difference, an ease with other people and other views. When the going gets tough, authenticity is even more important. "The concept of authenticity gains prominence in times when individuals facing conflicting social pressures become entrapped in moral dilemmas that are engendered by the complex evolution of modern civilization," observed one group of academics contemplating this subject. They went on to trace the evolution of our understanding of authenticity from a moral virtue (see the philosopher Kierkegaard and others), as a matter of making ethical choices (Heidegger, Sartre, and others), to authenticity as a trait or state and authenticity as an identity.[26]

While the evolution of the idea of authentic leadership can be debated—it brings in strands from psychology, sociology, and elsewhere—the expressed need for it is unmistakable. It is a reaction to the turmoil and change of modern life. Work and family institutions seem under threat. Recent geopolitical events have dramatically and tragically reinforced this sense of turmoil. As rates of change increase, individuals are ever more motivated to search for constancy and meaning. Welcome to reality.

Collaborative and networked

The traditional concept of the leader is the leader as hero (in the West at least). In this version of leadership

- the leader is the most important person in the organization
- the top *is* the top
- strategy comes from the top—everyone else implements
- change is steered from above and often resisted by those below
- leaders make decisions and allocate resources
- rewards go mostly to shareholders
- leadership is thrust upon those who thrust themselves on others

This approach recalls the exploits of the East India Company four hundred years ago as well as that of the Hudson Bay Company. However, that is now changing.

The emerging model of leadership we now see in global organizations is that of the engaging leader. This brand of leader

- helps others deliver the service to customers
- leads through a network
- allows people to solve problems which become big initiatives
- encourages problem-solving
- inspires and engages others based on wise appreciation
- builds leadership on trust earned through respect

An international German company worked hard on developing a global approach and local approach. The CEO of the company frequently met with his general managers to discuss ways of improving competitiveness, reducing costs, and centralizing services, while at the same time being flexible, meeting local needs, and giving the general managers considerable discretion on how to best integrate corporate requirements with local requirements. The corporation's approach was to trust its general managers to make local decisions that may go against corporate strategies, in favor of local needs as long as the philosophy of the company concerning competitiveness and costs was not undermined. This required frequent meetings between the regional general managers and the CEO, so that all could keep in touch with what was happening locally and globally.

This was a very successful approach: the general managers knew each other and each others' issues so well that they could get together and implement strategy in a way that was sensitive to local contexts without undermining the corporate strategy. All the general managers took a keen interest in each others' local concerns and territories. Yet, how many organizations can boast such capability? How many general managers are as interested in their colleague's business as their own?

Or consider a traditional industry—tobacco. It may not be every MBA graduate's dream job these days, but for all of its ethical dilemmas tobacco continues to be a major employer. Imperial Tobacco under the former leadership of Gareth Davies and Derek Bonham, respectively CEO and chairman, has devised merger and acquisition strategies which successfully repositioned the company from a relatively minor player into one of the most prominent global tobacco companies. The company's leadership philosophy is attuned to shareholder value, but the way it is implemented displays considerable sensitivity to different national and local contexts.

The great strength of Imperial Tobacco was and continues to be a robust, open, and transparent top team together with a similar and like-minded board. The company has championed talent, ensuring that the best people get the best jobs and on this basis had no problems redesigning its top management in order to introduce new talent from the organizations it acquired. As a result, clarity of philosophy; sensitivity concerning context; an open, transparent, and motivating leadership style, as well as rewards for talent, have made Imperial Tobacco one of the best run companies in the world. A testament to its strength is the fact that when it undertook an acquisition in Germany it was able to introduce a cost reduction program without any legal repercussions. Compare this with Wal-Mart's German experience discussed earlier.

Our modern global leader, then, is part corporate diplomat. For him or her, probably the most important skill is the ability to build a global network of relationships with other business leaders, diplomats, politicians, NGOs, customers, and suppliers. Without a network any global leader is effectively powerless.

Diplomacy requires the leader to answer the question *how* rather than *what*. The diplomatic leader must be able to get under the skin of the person they are negotiating with—even if they don't like them. Being filled with anger and rage does not achieve results. Effective global leaders are able to suppress negative energy and emotions and by focusing on achievable outcomes they are able to take action. In every encounter, at every meeting with another person, the leader must strive to be involved and empathetic if he or she wants positive outcomes.

Inevitably, the economic power vested in them means that global corporate leaders, who are not politicians or elected officials, increasingly have political clout. Their decisions influence the daily lives of people all over the world, whether intentionally or unintentionally. To pretend otherwise is disingenuous. Businesses and business leaders control knowledge, land, and know-how: the levers for the accumulation and concentration of power and wealth. Moreover, business leaders are continually influencing local businesses, governments, and other interested parties on mutual goals and benefits.

For example, U.S. multinationals may influence and even shape foreign policy toward the country in which they operate. But it isn't just corporations that are powerbrokers. Certain NGOs also have tremendous influence in developing countries— because they are large. Small NGOs are often at the mercy of large corporations because they are either directly or indirectly dependent on their money. All are led by nonelected officials.

A catalyst and developer

Global leaders often act like consultants to their own teams. They can switch from being a director to being a facilitator with impressive ease.

One of the big problems with leadership is actually getting the top team and the board to agree to a unified concept for the organization. Local concerns still have a tendency to hold sway, even in global organizations. In fact, this is probably the biggest problem in most businesses today. The Smirnoff example earlier was a classic example of this. How do we get a group of senior managers to stand above their job, see the corporate gain, and have the maturity to undertake certain actions, which go against local objectives, but hit corporate objectives?

Who would have the guts to say that in order to get this pharmaceutical onto the market as a global brand in Japan, what I want you to do is cut costs in this area and create a redundancy program of 5,000 people? Imagine how much harder this is when you're the Japanese manager who's been brought up with the very people you're going to make redundant. But these are the sorts of real challenges that face global leaders.

How do we get people to stand above their job, rethink their roles because of the skill of the leader and the economic logic of the strategy? What's the role of the CEO in this? What's the role of the chairman and board? How do the board directors become sufficiently in tune with the business to understand how to make assessment of a merger and acquisition and what integration means once we've acquired this company, so that we understand how to realize that competitive advantage? Such fundamentals require that leaders are catalysts for change and developers of further change.

Passionate and rational

The vision of the future does not need to be nailed down to the smallest detail. Events dictate that the best-laid plans can unravel. There are no watertight five-year plans any more (in reality there never were). This is as it should be. No leader has a monopoly on wisdom. No board has all the answers. No chairman is omniscient.

Displaying a passion for the mission is exciting and infectious. Others voluntarily push themselves to succeed through performing beyond expectations.

We have learned a great deal about passion from the former trade union leader, social reformer and politician, Tom Sawyer. Now, Lord Sawyer, he insightfully redesigned the United Kingdom's Labour Party headquarters providing a strong platform for Tony Blair's reforms. As comfortable with sorting out labor disputes as with working through top management wrangles, Tom has chaired the boards of public service agencies and private sector enterprises alike. He believes that there is one fundamental factor which has to be in place to achieve compatibility of thinking at board and top team level: passion for the mission. People have to believe. Passion begins at the top.

Of course, the reverse also applies. Where there is no passion, it is unlikely that the chairman will be able to transmit belief to those around him or her. Tom Sawyer recalls one appointment which didn't work out and that was because, he explains, "I did not feel some level of passion about what the organization stood for."[27]

Desire, coupled with a logic that rationally justifies the next steps to be taken, provides for a common platform of understanding and the will to act. "Look carefully and calmly and say I really do think that it is very worthwhile doing. I think I can add value to the organization," concludes Tom Sawyer. Tom recalls the chief executive of Marriot Hotels telling an audience that there was only one way for them to find out if he was doing his job properly—when they went to their hotel bedrooms was the toilet paper neatly turned up? "The chief executive is in New York and wants to know the woman in Hong Kong who cleans the bedroom knows what do to. The principle is good," says Tom Sawyer. "As a chairman, I ask myself what's the toilet roll test in this business?"[28]

Ask Yourself

- How do you define leadership?
- Are you a global leader? If not, why not?
- How do you set priorities in hectic times?
- How do you alter your leadership when you work in different places?
- How do you give credit to people?
- Which of the characteristics of global leaders do you need to work at?
- What's the toilet roll test in your business?

Negotiate the gray areas of governance

Global leaders recognize that right and wrong can vary with context. They are able to move from black and white to gray.

Tiers and a frown

A company we came across is known as one of the most ethical German companies. It is deeply concerned about its people and the community. The secretary to the board came to us and said he had an awful problem. In Germany there is a two-tier board structure with a management board and a board of directors. The company's management board had announced that it did not tolerate corruption and hence would not discuss corruption at board level. Having heard this, certain general managers across the world came back to the secretary and said when I'm caught, what will you do? And the answer had to be, if you're caught, you must be guilty and it's not a company problem. The secretary to the board was troubled because it simply wasn't true. "The reality is you pay now for the contract. So if a contract is worth £2 billion, £200 million of that contract immediately goes to paying people to make sure that you get a contract of 1.8 billion. These are not the poor operatives and so on. These are governments, ministers. It is institutionalized corruption. What do I do? Do I stand up and honestly put this guy who's been working in this company in prison saying that we had no knowledge of this when we did?"

Of course, the official position is that the company leaves the errant manager to take the flak. This, patently, isn't fair. But it happens and, until these issues are discussed, will continue to do so.

Trouble unlimited

Let's begin with a roll call of the corporate world's hall of shame: Think back to the $Aus 25 million Nugan Hand Bank scandal in Australia in 1980; Polly Peck's travails in 1990 in the United Kingdom when the CEO eventually fled the country; the falsifying of financial results which hit Xerox and KPMG in 2000; Enron in 2001; inflated revenues reported at Bristol Myers Squibb in 2002; inflated revenues at Qwest; understated liabilities at Nicor; misleading accounting practices at Kmart; improper accounting at Tyco International; falsified accounting documents at Parmalat; and that of Satyam, India (outsourcing) whose CEO resigned earlier in 2009 on the basis of profits being falsely inflated, through to the toxic debts of the great credit crunch.

Bribery and corruption are extensive. Fraud within the United Kingdom's financial industry costs the country around £14 billion every year. In addition, £25 billion is reported to be laundered by British institutions.[29]

Since 1995, Transparency International has published an annual Corruption Perceptions Index ordering the countries of the world according to "the degree to which corruption is perceived to exist among public officials and politicians." The organization defines corruption as "the abuse of entrusted power for private gain." The poll covers 180 countries. A higher score means less (perceived) corruption. The results show that 129 out of 180 countries score 5 points or less out of 10.

In the 2008 index Denmark, New Zealand, and Sweden (each scoring 9.3) were the countries least perceived as corrupt. At the other end of the scale, the index indicates that there is a strong link between poverty and corruption, with Somalia, Iraq, Myanmar, and Haiti perceived as most corrupt according to Transparency International.[30]

Gray backs

So, if you're a U.S. company dealing with China you can bury your corporate head in the sand or you have to learn how to deal with bribery and corruption. That's a big issue. We estimate, from having been to China many times, that some 450 million people who work in China accept bribes at some point in their lives. Chinese and Western managers have told us that Western companies routinely bribe four or five times a week if they are doing business in China. This may be what the Chinese call "gray money" or simply allowing people to siphon off their share of a deal.

In China, gray money is part of life. Increasingly the Chinese are becoming more confident to talk openly about gray money. It works simply: a manager accepts a "friendly payment" and then distributes it to the appropriate people. If you fail to distribute gray money you end up in trouble. This is often the real reason why managers are brought to trial for corruption. (The other standard reason is that the manager has politically fallen out of favor.)

And, as we have seen, it is not just China. We had a friend who was working for a British company. He was a managing director of a subsidiary and he sent his senior manager to go to Italy to sort out an IT contract. The senior manager came back and said he'd had to stop negotiations because the Italian manager he was dealing with wanted to use part of the money for the deal for the British company to build an entirely new kitchen in his house. The managing director went over to sort the matter out and then called to ask for our advice: he was now being asked to also build a kitchen for the managing director of the Italian firm. So, two kitchens instead of one and all because of trying to be honest.

At one extreme, bribery is simply paying a brokerage fee for a transaction. It happens everywhere, even paying for services through brown paper envelopes on the streets of London.

We talked to an entrepreneur who wanted to locate a renewable energy business that would provide local jobs in an area of England. The local airport was managed by a councilor who could affect the planning decision on the wind farm. The airport needed a new radar system and asked the entrepreneur for money as a display of his sense of community spirit. He refused and the application was not approved.

In a sense both sides in this were in the right. The airport was a vital community resource and improvements would have benefited the community. But should they have been so clearly tied to a planning application? Probably not. As it stands, however, both sides lost out. Win:win became lose:lose.

When's a bribe a bribe?

The reality is that the world is more pragmatic than we might like to think. Companies with killer products tend to have high ethical standards. Companies selling commodities have to get on with local markets on local terms.

The big problem is not the grayness of so many of our transactions, but of our holier-than-thou unwillingness to acknowledge their grayness. People in the West, in particular, tend to see the world in black and white when it is actually a rainbow of hues of gray.

For example, you may go to New York, have a lovely meal, and tip the waiter. Why do you tip the waiter and why does that waiter get angry if you don't tip or tip less than the 17½ or 20 percent they expect? The answer is that you the customer, the proprietor, and the waiter are in a relationship, which bolsters the waiter's wages. You are not tipping for service, but providing a necessary addition to the waiter's living, daily wage. It is morally acceptable to underpay a New York waiter, but only because we tip.

In London, we leave tips but our assumption is that the waiter is paid adequately. So why do we tip?—supposedly for excellent service. In Japan, tipping is actually an insult. Waiters are paid already so you do not need to tip them because it is their job to provide the highest level of service. In China you don't tip but make a friendly payment.

Now, we have been to New York and sat at a table with an American tax inspector who tipped cash. We asked him whether the waiter was likely to declare the income and, if not, how could he as an American tax inspector give him cash in the knowledge that he was unlikely to declare it? "Yes, but that's America," said the inspector. So if an American tax inspector behaves like that why don't we have sympathy for the Chinese who simply have taken the practice of tipping from service industries to basically every other industry?

In fact, the idea of a friendly payment—a contractual relationship, which shows concern for the other—is now much more common practice than the Anglo-American approach. In Germany it accounts for approximately 1.7 to 1.8 billion euros annually. It is also commonplace in Italy, Indonesia, Mexico, Brazil, China, Malaysia, Turkey, Greece, former Soviet satellite states like Kazakhstan, as well as a number of South American countries. The only people that don't basically do it as a daily practice are the British, Americans, the Irish, Scandinavians, Australians, and New Zealanders.

If you look at the world, the Anglo-Americans are actually trying to do something that is completely counter-cultural and has a limited chance of surviving. Of course, the alternative is to pay people a decent wage.

Accept the grayness

Michael Payne is the former marketing director of the International Olympic Committee who spent 20 years negotiating broadcast and sponsorship deals for the Olympics. The most controversial of these concerned the 2008 Beijing Olympic Games.

"You cannot nail down every detail of a long-term relationship in a contract. There will always be grey areas. You have to be prepared to deal with the inevitable issues these create as and when they emerge. Flexibility is essential if you are to build long-term relationships," says Payne. "At times, it comes down less to what the contract says but whether an action enhances and supports the Olympic brand and strengthens the partnership for the future. This is not always a popular strategy with the IOC lawyers but it works.

The second grey area is that the Olympic brand will always attract people with their own agenda. For example, it was simply unrealistic to imagine that the Beijing Games would not bring its own ethical challenges, not least an entire grey market in Olympic merchandising. Burying your head in the sand is not a viable strategy. The long-term protection of the Olympic brand requires its custodians to engage with the grey areas."[31]

Payne concludes that there are times, not often but occasionally, when it is necessary to bend the rules. The key to this is recognizing that rules are not the same as principles. The fundamental Olympic principles remain untouchable.

Take this example from the 1996 Atlanta Olympic Games. Claudia Poll from Costa Rica won the women's 200-meter freestyle. It was her country's first ever gold medal. The flag of Costa Rica looks remarkably like the logo of Pepsi Cola—a red, white and blue wave. Everyone thought that Poll was swimming with a head cap proudly bearing the national flag. But close examination of press photographs revealed that the cap was an advertisement for Pepsi.

Costa Rica was in uproar claiming that Coca-Cola had brought the matter to the IOC's attention, and that because of Coke, Costa Rica would now lose its gold medal. Coke knew nothing about the issue, until the IOC began investigating, and was torn between, on the one hand, wanting the IOC to come down hard on such a blatant case of ambush marketing, and on the other not taking the rap in Costa Rica and seeing its market share collapse through an incident that it had nothing to do with.

In the end, after a formal apology from the Costa Rican Olympic Committee, it was decided that in view of the fact that this was the country's first ever medal, the IOC would not press for the ultimate sanction. Ms Poll was not allowed to compete again wearing similar headgear, but was allowed to keep her medal.

Governance underground

How we do business and the standards applied to business vary from country to country, region to region. Take governance.

Governance is 101 things across the world. The Higgs Combined Code simply applies in Britain. It means little in Japan, China, or Germany. Sarbanes-Oxley is legislation for the United States and the United States imposes that discipline on businesses that want to do business with its organizations. So if you are a Chinese executive, you better know how to deal with Sarbanes-Oxley's procedures if you're trading in the United States.

Western business people bridle at the notion of grayness and point enthusiastically to the governance regulations, which occupy the minds and time of CEOs and directors. The mistaken assumption is that Western governance codes mean Western businesses are above reproach. Not so. A number of U.S. external directors are of the opinion that Sarbanes-Oxley, brought in after the series of corporate scandals at the start of the decade, has induced even greater inhibition at board level and, as one suggested, "may even be driving corruption more underground."

Approached with a more positive frame of mind, regulation can be used as an opportunity to introduce valuable disciplines into enterprises. That view is now more readily supported.

"It's not Sarbanes that is suffocating businesses. It's Sarbanes done badly," observes Jonathan Wyatt, managing director of Protiviti, a risk consultancy. "A lot of businesses didn't understand the requirements and didn't know where they were going, so they introduced a new form to be filled out and that becomes a major pain."[32]

World-class organizations emphasize being *more* than compliant. Be ahead of the game is the best advice. The rules of the game are constantly being refined. Whatever the rules, governance must be for longevity. There should be no debate about that point.

Your world view isn't my world view

Grayness meets governance when it comes to executive pay. Some statistics. The average remuneration of a European top executive—including stock options, salary, and bonuses—comes to around 5 million euros a year. Total compensation for Deutsche Bank CEO Josef Ackermann was listed as €1,389,586 for 2008, by *Forbes* magazine.

In America the average is some 13 million euros. For example, Oracle CEO Larry Ellison was reported as earning some $84 million in 2008, although that includes stock, which will take time to mature (however he also cashed out stock options worth several hundred million dollars).

There are regular complaints in Europe that executive pay is spiraling out of control. Jean-Claude Juncker, prime minister of Luxembourg and president of the group of European finance ministers, has lamented "scandalous" abuses in executive pay and labeled it obscene, bizarre, a social scourge. Meanwhile, in the United States huge payments to corporate leaders are largely accepted.

Warren Buffett reportedly referred to executive compensation as "the acid test" of U.S. corporate reform. The *Financial Times* highlights, "One of the problems with measuring progress in the field of executive pay is that the gauges used are at best crude, at worst, open to dispute."[33] The very essence of executive remuneration, assessing performance, is open to substantial dispute. Controversy surrounds CEO performance when related to increases in shareholder value and the meeting of shareholder expectations.

An interesting development on this is the interest taken by President Obama. Since taking office, he has set up a number of committees to look at corporate governance issues. One important aspect he identifies is the question of whether the role of the CEO and chairman should be split. While this division of roles is resisted on principle in many parts of corporate America, Obama has indicated that in his eyes the issue is less about a principle—and more concerned with how it is being practiced. If the roles are to be changed, something will first have to change in the relative remuneration of CEOs and chairmen—American chairmen currently receive relatively low rewards for high levels of responsibility.

The issue of executive pay is not going to go away. To echo Warren Buffett's point, how a company deals with difficult issues such as executive pay is also the acid test of its leadership. A world-class company faces the issues head on—and develops an approach that can be legitimized.

Linking executive pay with performance seems the obvious solution. But the three ultimate goals of shareholder value, competitive advantage and differentiation, sit uncomfortably side by side. Add to this, stakeholder considerations, then achieving strategic alignment is even more stretching. How can excessive pay be awarded when such alignment is not forthcoming?

Despite all other innovations, stock options remain a prime lever for linking personal performance with corporate performance. Stock options have attracted comment ranging from concerned critique to plain abuse. The *Financial Times* reports shareholder activists who estimate the pay difference between the average operative against the average CEO in the United States as 300:1.[34] Attracta Lagan and Brian Moran, in their book *3D Ethics*, dispute the comparator as derisory and offer the sum of 4,589 times greater than the take-home pay of the average American worker.[35]

All this begs the question of where fair pay ends and overcompensation begins. Pfizer's CEO Hank McKinnell, for example, received a lump sum retirement benefit of $83 million for 35 years' service, a projected $6.5 million in retirement pay per year. That was more than his $2.27 million salary. Not surprisingly, shareholders questioned the value gained from their CEO when Pfizer shares dropped by approximately 43 percent over recent years.[36]

Of course, one of the difficulties with linking performance and pay is that the effects on performance of improved operations—whether as a result of restructuring, outsourcing, introducing new products and equipment, and so on—are not instant. There is always a time lag. This makes it extremely difficult to prove a hard and fast relationship between what the CEO did last year and his level of remuneration.

Who knows best whether the remuneration package appropriately includes reward for taking charge of long-term change unlikely to be visible for quite some time? Again, only the board of the company.

In our view the issue with CEO remuneration should be: what is this job worth? For example, if you are charged with transforming an airline then perhaps you should be paid more than a CEO who is simply operating a successful business.

Clearly and openly specifying the reasoning behind any top executive's remuneration, drawing on immediate performance, as well as future gain effects, displays integrity. The politics of remuneration are as important a consideration as the details of the package. Perhaps we should look more objectively at what an individual's job actually is and, as a result, what it is worth. Otherwise grayness rules yet again.

Standard setting

To some extent the Western view is that we've got to educate the world. Whether it is pollution or child labor someone has to take a lead, someone has to say that's not acceptable.

This is laudable, but the challenge is that the Anglo-American shareholder culture is basically contractual. In contrast the German, French, Italian, Greek, Turkish, Chinese, Indonesian, Mexican, and most South American stakeholder cultures are about relationships. Their networks are much more important regulators than their governments.

So, what's the big issue, for example, on a German board? It is not how much you've earned. On a German board, it's on how many other boards you sit and don't declare. If you're on my board, you might sit on a competitors board, or be driven by that network. But how do I know then that you're not giving this company's strategy to that cluster of interrelationships? The answer is trust and trust in the German culture is firmly built on relationships.

Certain American and British companies do very well in China because they formed the right linkages with government. They have talked to government about how to invest in the universities, their local communities, and support worthwhile initiatives. They have gone out of their way to understand what the local context is about and they've integrated it into their business practice. These companies combine excellence of product and service, excellence of employee benefits and sustainable performance and investment in that community. There is no grayness to excellence.

Ask Yourself

- Is there a shared view concerning the governance issues facing the organization?
- Are the top team and the board involved in that debate—or is it just left to the board?
- Are gray areas even discussed? What actions arise from discussions of these issues?
- How are the governance gray areas reconciled with protecting your corporate reputation?

Network like crazy ... and globally

The network is the thing. Quality of relationships and networking is often more important than squeezing out cost. The challenge is to put effectiveness above efficiency. Who do you know?

What is a network?

With the surfeit of events, breakfasts, organizations and online websites dedicated to networking, you could be forgiven for thinking that networking is a relatively new concept. But of course networking has been with us for thousands of years, as evidenced by the arch-networking of the elite of the Roman Empire as they manipulated and networked their way into positions of power.

Throughout history, business leaders, too, have built empires and fashioned careers through the careful cultivation of contacts, informally and formally, in the banquet hall, on the golf course, and in the boardroom.

Take the example of Lord Beaverbrook, one of the twentieth century's most successful media magnates. In 1910 Lord Beaverbrook arrived in England from Canada, as plain William Maxwell Aitken, a successful businessman looking to make his way in a new country. Using his formidable networking skills, Aitken became a member of parliament the year he arrived. Within a short time his network of contacts included three future prime ministers in Lloyd George, Andrew Bonar Law, and Winston Churchill. He became Lord Beaverbrook in 1917.

Alfred Sloan, one of General Motors' most celebrated CEOs, was another leader who understood the importance of mingling with the customers. Once a year GM would hold a big party, know as its "frictionless feast," in reference to the company's smooth auto bearings. With the industry great and good descending on GM, Sloan took soundings from customers and competitors, such as Henry Ford and the Dodge brothers.

In more modern times, Scott McNealy, the founder of tech giant Sun Microsystems, engaged in some high-profile networking when he challenged Jack Welch, General Electric's legendary former CEO, to a round of golf. McNealy lost, but so impressed Welch that he offered him a place on the GE board.

For modern business executives networking remains a core competence, a competence that might be viewed in terms of relationship management, aided by personal skills, and manifest in the building and maintaining of networks, partnerships, and alliances, both inside and outside an organization, in a personal and professional capacity, and across national, regional and continental boundaries.

Note too that networking is both good for your career and your personal development. It forces the prone-to-shyness executive to move out of their comfort zone. And that is a good thing because researchers have shown that people who are shy tend to begin their careers later than non-shy people, are more apt to refuse promotions, choose careers that are less interpersonal, are more undecided about which field to pursue, and have a harder time developing a career identity.[37]

Networks of influence

The importance of networks and personal relationship cannot be overemphasized. The strength of your personal relationship forms the underlying social content of your business relationship.

In the West people refer to *business friends*. These are people with whom you have little interaction outside of work, a limited knowledge base, and some self-disclosure. In contrast, there are *strictly business relationships* where there is no personal interaction or communication, no self-disclosure and no personal knowledge base, and the relationship is focused on the project. At the other extreme are *personal relationships* characterized by highly intimate self-disclosure, significant interaction outside of work, and a fully developed knowledge base.

Bonding is a critical component in how interpersonal relationships develop. In Western cultures with a high structural orientation (individualism) there is more emphasis on structural bonding while Eastern cultures with a high interpersonal orientation (collectivism) put more emphasis on social bonding—the shared degree of mutual personal friendship and liking.

Highly intimate self-disclosure, significant interaction outside of work, a fully developed knowledge base, strong emotional attachment and shared commitment and personal loyalty create a deep relationship. In the Chinese context this is referred to as *guanxi* (relationships) based on, *xinren*, or deep trust, and in the Saudi Arabian and Gulf States context, this type of relationship is referred to as *et-moon*, which literally means "whatever I have is yours; you can do whatever you like without my permission." That is seen as a positive and borderless relationship, with no formalities or restrictions with the highest possible level of mutual interdependency, trust, commitment, and cooperation.

Terms such as friendship, social reputation, personal recognition, and liking lie at the heart of business relationships but have different meanings and emphases. In China managers are more willing to honor a deal as friendship is more valuable than the deal itself. However, ensuring relationship continuity is tied primarily to the family rather than the business firm. This is in sharp contrast to the West, but in most ancient cultures the personal relationships are essential to commercial exchanges.

Right clubbing

Some networks open more doors than others. This explains the enduring appeal of exclusive clubs. Businesspeople have always been a clubbable lot, but the networking-obsessed new economy spawns new possibilities.

Clubs have a long history. The nineteenth century was the heyday of gentlemen's clubs in Britain. Victoria may have been on the throne but women were rarely included in the power networks of the day. Over time, the gentlemen were joined by the new barons of business and commerce. The newcomers brought a commercial agenda. In places such as the Athenaeum, the Carlton, and the Reform Club, political debate gave way to more pragmatic concerns. The idea that the vulgar conduct of business should be left at the door was wasted on the new arrivals.

The club as business model appeals to others. For serious network effect, the Global Business Network (GBN) is hard to beat. Founded by scenario-planning guru and former Shell executive Peter Schwartz and four friends in 1987, the idea emerged around a pool table in a Berkeley, California, basement. The five co-founders envisioned a worldwide learning community of organizations and individuals. GBN's Explorers Club is there to help companies "transition from the old to the new economy."

In return for their GBN membership cards, thrusting executives get the chance to hob-nob with each other at seminars and conferences, picking up lots of fresh ideas and perspectives on the way. They belong to an exclusive club that includes business gurus, show biz doyens, and a former Apollo astronaut.

Leading GBN members and advisers include the management luminaries Michael Porter, Gary Hamel, Esther Dyson, Edgar Schein, and Arie de Geus. Bill Joy, co-founder of Sun Microsystems is another GBN member, as is John Kao, author of *Jamming* and founder of The Idea factory. Kevin Kelly of *Wired* magazine, and artists including Brian Eno, Peter Gabriel, and the novelist Douglas Coupland are also GBN members or advisory members.

Education, too, remains a prime source of exclusivity. For example, whilst 7 percent of the UK population attends private schools, 75 percent of judges and 45 percent of top civil servants are privately educated.[38] However, the traditional power networks—Ivy League, Oxbridge, Grand Ecoles—are being augmented by business schools. Business schools are taking the educational club to new heights.

The B-schools alumni clubs are among the most powerful executive clubs. They help graduates develop their careers, update skills, make new contacts—and generally open doors in the world of business, politics, and beyond. At the bigger and better-known schools, the alumni networks are worldwide fellowships. From Boston to Beijing, and most cities in between, there will be a member of the alumni network who is only too pleased to make alumni feel at home.

Cranfield School of Management's alumni association, the Cranfield Management Association (CMA) illustrates how alumni networks can benefit students. "During the MBA, the CMA was instrumental in arranging networking events and topical presentations from lecturers and guest speakers at Cranfield and in London," says Bill Toong one Cranfield MBA graduate. "This allowed students to tap into a ready-made pool of knowledge and experience. Thus, in addition to the 'learning' from the MBA, I have an ongoing network that I can both contribute to, and that will assist in my future endeavours."

As well as arranging networking events, Cranfield alumni regularly return to the school to hold mock job interviews, provide projects for the students, run case studies, and even act as assessors. The CMA also taps into its network of approximately 9,000 graduates for job vacancies, often previously unadvertised, which are posted onto the CMA website daily.

With more than 60,000 active alumni worldwide, in terms of pure networking muscle Harvard Business School is in a class of its own. At one point it was calculated that no fewer than a quarter of the directors of the Fortune 500 companies were Harvard alumni.

In a business world of ambiguity and alienation, clubs and networks offer certainty and a sense of belonging. That isn't going to change. If you can't beat them, better have your check book at the ready.

Plugged into the network

Of course, like most everything else, modern technology and especially the internet has changed the way that we network. With the advent of Web 2.0, so-called online networking has come of age with "social networking"—witness the intermittent emails from people you know, barely know, or have no idea who they are, exhorting you to "join their network."

Near the top of the pile of online networking firms, alongside the likes of the ubiquitous Facebook, is LinkedIn, founded by chairman and president, Reid Hoffman. Hoffman, a leading light in the internet firmament, has a stellar technology track record, that includes stints at Apple Computer, Fujitsu, and PayPal, and has been described as the "most connected man in all of Silicon Valley." A serial internet investor he spends a lot of the time circumnavigating the planet.

The initial idea for LinkedIn, says Hoffman, was that every professional should have a profile on the web, so that other people could find them.

Now Hoffman explains the premise for LinkedIn as follows: "We all have a set of people that we work with and have good relationships of trust and exchange with. Although LinkedIn allows you to approach people you don't know, it is more about staying in touch with professional, current and former colleagues and classmates; finding the right kind of professional information to help solve problems and perform tasks; and finding the right people that can help you succeed in business."

Demonstrating the global nature of the social networking phenomenon, Hoffman relates a story about the website. "One executive needed to know the best way to move 12 million tons of cement from China to Dubai," he says. "He posted the question on LinkedIn, and within 24 hours got an answer pointing him to the right expert in order to solve that problem. On average when people post questions, they get about seven answers, a huge majority of which are helpful and high quality."

So people get to create virtual networks of contacts—or connections. Some go for volume—open networks. Some go for trust—trust-based networks. Hoffman says both work, but in different ways.

CEO Coach, and CEO of Change-Leaders.com, Marjan Bolmeijer has spent many years refining her approach to networking and, more recently, her use of social networking websites and online communities. A big fan of LinkedIn, Bolmeijer is in the top 20 networks by size (as of April 2009) with first level connection numbering over 26,000.[39]

That's comparatively small fry compared with Ron Bates, managing principal of Executive Advance Group, and probably the most networked man on the planet. Bates boasts over 44,000 connections (many more by the time this goes to print, no doubt). It is not known if he phones them all on a regular basis.

These kinds of numbers may be out of reach of many, and of practical use to only a few, but Bolmeijer makes an important point about the numbers.

"It might seem like a high number, but at certain times, when you need your network the most, when you are in transition and looking for a new position, for example, that network can turn out to be really small," she says.

Bolmeijer has some tips for social network users. Never change your phone number, or your email address, she says. Make sure your email address goes next to your name, and put as much information about yourself in your profile as possible. She also cautions against messing up—bad news travels fast through your network.

Remember, also, she says, networking is not just about give and take and adding value, ultimately you have to get to the point with people where you really like each other, and there is a level of trust. Then people want to do business with you.

Cultural networking

Networking comes with cultural obstacles attached, partly because it involves some very basic elements, whether it is the language, or the way you communicate.

The cultural differences are a bonus for some people. Like Buddy Ye, for instance, founder of WangYou, a social networking website in China. Ask Ye whether he fears competition from the likes of Facebook, MySpace, or LinkedIn and Ye is sanguine about the threat.

"We have some advantages over competition from the main players, because we are a local company staffed by local Chinese people," he says. "This business is very culturally sensitive. You need to be able to understand the local culture very deeply; it is not just about language, for example."[40]

For the rest of us who are trying to build networks with fellow executives across cultures, the different approaches become more problematic.

In Japan, for example, even meeting other people has a formalized process. Unless there has been a formal exchange of business cards, the meetings should be arranged via a trusted common acquaintance in the first instance. Only after the acquaintance has made the initial contact are you then able to contact the person directly to arrange a meeting.

Bear in mind, however, that there is an important culture of obligation and fulfillment of obligation in Japan. And so an executive may find that the person they wish to meet agrees to do so only out of obligation to the common acquaintance, and not from any idea to do business!

In India, networking requires careful consideration of the family relationships as many networks in India are based on familial connections.

The Chinese are keen networkers, we know this from personal experience. One Chinese leader we knew had a network of 10,000 people. And this wasn't through Facebook. These were people he knew and actively cultivated. They were all aware that they were part of his network.

In China preservation of a critical relationship is all important, resulting in continual repositioning within networks. Understanding networking in China means understanding relationships, and understanding "face" (divided into *mian*—social status and prestige—and *liǎn*—being perceived as someone who behaves in a morally correct manner within society).

In China, everything is about "face." You can trade your face, save your face, save your friend's face, even borrow face. If I ask favor of you, I am borrowing your face. "Give me a face," I could ask you. Give me a face means please go and talk on my behalf to somebody else. So you gain me a face, and I now owe you a face, next time you ask me for a favor, I have to do something for you. So it's all about trading the face.

Keep networking

Regardless of cultural differences there is one universal truth about networking. You need to keep doing it. Networks need maintaining, otherwise they become passive. Constantly update and develop your network of contacts. If your network is out of date or out of power, you are out of date and out of favor.

We have a friend in Cyprus who is a mid-ranking telecoms operative. We get a call from him on our birthdays every year, and are always pleased to hear from him because he is an enormously warm and extremely likeable man. More than that, he has made it his business to know the birthdays of a large number of people. This is his network. As a result, Nicoli can ring up everyone from members of royal families to many in the European Parliament. Now that is networking!

When Andrew was talking to the Irish entrepreneur Sir Tony O'Reilly about a matter relating to South Africa he remarked: "I called Nelson." He meant Nelson Mandela and he was absolutely serious. Think about it: who will take your phone call? Will a minister of state interrupt a meeting to talk to you?

Networking is a daily commitment, not a monthly social activity. Success requires that executives must become more efficient users of their networks. Networking is the cornerstone of good management wherever you may be—or want to be.

Ask Yourself

- How far reaching is your network?
- Can you as easily ring a friend as a minister of state?
- How well do you leverage your network?
- How do you balance day-to-day tasks with networking activities?

Notes

1. "Chinese grown Starbucks coffee: The next big thing?" *Shanghaiist,* January 15, 2009,
2. http://money.cnn.com/magazines/fortune/global500/2008/full_list/
3. http://web.worldbank.org/WBSITE/EXTERNAL/TOPICS/EXTPOVERTY/E XTPA/0,,contentMDK:20153855~menuPK:435040~pagePK:148956~piPK:2166 18~theSitePK:430367,00.html
4. Crainer, Stuart and Dearlove, Des, (2008)"Gain the world, lose your soul?" *Conference Board Review,* November/December. Other examples from this article are used with the permission of the authors.
5. Ibid.
6. "Swiss suffer secrecy loss to sustain money management," Bloomberg News, March 6, 2009.
7. Ohmae, Kenichi (2005) *The Next Global Stage,* Wharton Publishing, New Jersey.
8. Brown, Tom (2007) "Where business and politics meet," *Business Strategy Review,* Winter.
9. Kurzweil, Ray (2006) *The Singularity Is Near,* Gerald Duckworth & Company, London, UK.
10. Snyder, Thomas A. (2008) "Complexipacity: Assessing one's capacity for complexity," unpublished article, www.momentsintimeexhibits.com.
11. Compiled from Richmond, B. (1997) "The thinking in systems thinking," *The Systems Thinker,* Vol. 8, No. 2.
12. Ashby, W. R. (1956) *Introduction to Cybernetics,* Chapman & Hall, London, UK; Ashby, W. R. (1958) *Requisite Variety and Its Implications for the Control of Complex Systems,* Cybernetica (Namur) Vol. 1, No. 2.
13. Interview with Des Dearlove, www.thinkers50.com, accessed March 3, 2009.
14. Kakabadse, Andrew and Kakabadse, Nada (2008) *Leading the Board: The Six Disciplines of World Class Chairmen,* Palgrave Macmillan, London.
15. Prahalad, C. K. and Ooserveld, Jan (1999) "Transforming internal governance," *Sloan Management Review,* Spring.
16. Kelly, L. Kevin (2008) *Top Jobs,* Wharton Business Press, New Jersey.
17. Tyson, Laura and Andrews, Nigel (2004) "Global business capabilities," *Business Strategy Review,* Winter.

18. Micklethwait, John and Wooldridge, Adrian (2000) *A Future Perfect,* Crown, New York.

19. Dearlove, Des (2007) "Marshall calling," *Business Strategy Review,* Winter.

20. Bartlett, C. and Ghoshal, S. (2003) "What is a global manager?" *Harvard Business Review,* Vol. 81, No. 6.

21. Deanne, N. D. H. (2003) "What indeed do managers do?" *The Leadership Quarterly,* 14.

22. Wren, J. T. (1995) *Leader's Companion: Insights on Leadership through the Ages,* The Free Press, New York.

23. Greenleaf.org (2002) What is servant-leadership? Robert K. Greenleaf Center for Servant-Leadership website:http://www.greenleaf.org/leadership/servant-leadership/What-is-Servant-Leadership.html

24. Spears, L. C. (2002) *On Character and Servant-Leadership: Ten Characteristics of Effective, Caring Leaders.* Robert K. Greenleaf Center for Servant-Leadership Website:http://www.greenleaf.org/leadership/read-about-it/articles/On-Character-and-Servant-Leadership-Ten-Characteristics.html

25. Kakabadse, A., Kakabadse, N., and Lee-Davis, L., (2007) "Three temptation of leaders," *Leadership and Organisational Development Journal,* Vol. 28, No. 3, pp. 196–208.

26. Novicevic, Milorad; Harvey, Michael; Buckley, M. Ronald; Brown-Radford, Jo Ann; and Evans, Randy (2006) "Authentic leadership: A historical perspective," *Journal of Leadership and Organizational Studies,* Vol. 13, No. 1.

27. Kakabadse, Andrew and Kakabadse, Nada (2008) *Leading the Board: The Six Disciplines of World Class Chairmen,* Palgrave Macmillan, London.

28. Ibid.

29. "Watchdog warns of criminal gangs inside banks," *The Guardian,* November 16, 2005.

30. www.transparency.org/policy_research/surveys_indices/cpi

31. Payne, Michael (2005) *Olympic Turnaround,* London Business Press.

32. Jopson, B. (2006), "Pain Blamed on US red tape zealots eager to tick boxes. Accounting Standards", *Financial Times,* National News Business and Economy, Monday July 10, p. 3.

33. The Warren Buffett comment is taken from Hill, A. (2006) "Pay and the boardroom benchmark," *Financial Times,* Monday, July 10, p. 17.

34. Ibid.

35. For further information on the pay differences between CEOs and operatives, see Lagan, A. and Moran, B. (2006) *3D Ethics: Personal, Corporate, Social: Implementing Workplace Values,* Content Management, Maleny, Queensland, Australia, p. 32.

36. For further information on Pfizer's CEO pay and the questions it has raised, see Bowe, C., "Pfizer chief's pay scrutinised," *Financial Times,* Companies in America, Thursday, April 27, p. 26, 2006.

37. Azar, Beth (1995) "When self awareness works overtime." *APA Monitor,* November.

38. Unleashing Aspiration- the final report of the Panel on Fair Access to the Professions (2009). www.cabinetoffice.gov.uk/accessprofessions

39. www.toplinked.com/top50.html

40. Coomber, S. (2008) "Net Friend," *Business at Oxford,* No. 13, Summer, pp. 8–9.

PART II

Readiness

Triple R Global Leader

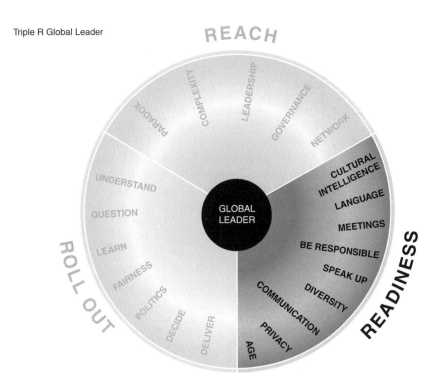

It is not the strongest of the species that survives, nor the most intelligent, but the one most responsive to change.

Attributed to Charles Darwin

Acquire cultural intelligence

Failure to understand a particular culture can prove expensive. The best global leaders are culturally sensitive.

Dining room

We hosted a group of friends for a dinner overlooking Sydney's wonderful harbor. Our guests were well-known business leaders from the United Kingdom, Australia, New Zealand, and America. The evening started well. All were of comparable status and worldly experience. But, the positive atmosphere was soon lost. The Englishman bristled at the Australians. The reason was not clear at first. Perhaps it was the Australian accent, or their more informal manner. It might have been the fact that the Australians were extremely insightful about world trends, open and honest about the reality of corruption in global business circles (of which the Englishman was a member). Also they held little respect for status. Probably it was the implicit critique of elites that most irritated our English guest.

In any group, irritations occur. What was interesting was that as soon as the Australians recognized the Englishman's discomfort, their style changed. They listened to him showing deep respect and tried their best to make him feel comfortable. The exquisite manner of the Australians was sorely tested when the Englishman declared he found Australian culture difficult to relate to.

"Just what is so fantastic about Australian indigenous art?" posed the Englishman. There was not even a reaction from the Australians. Instead, they talked about different cultures across the world and yes, it was difficult to relate to some especially when comparing European with non-European art and music. The sensitive, good manners of the Australians was further demonstrated when the Englishman talked about his own cultural background which the Australians knew little about but showed great interest in wanting to learn more.

So the evening turned out to be success. The Australians exhibited the essence of the global mind-set, a worldly curiosity with sensitivity for locality. The Englishman for all his clever words exhibited myopia. Not only was he insensitive to the local cosmos, but also equally ignorant. He showed no desire to learn.

Most of the time, the New Zealander and the American were uncomfortable and painfully smiled when the conversation veered toward what they regarded as intolerably sensitive. These two guests undoubtedly had worldly intellects, but not the EQ (emotional intelligence) necessary for sensitive global negotiation.

As our experience suggests, one can easily detect a global mind-set at dinner. By the end of the entrée, one's mind-set, global or local, is visible. One's emotional capacity to work through interesting tensions with competent people clearly shows itself. What counts is the quality of conversation by the time the cheese and biscuits arrive. It is worth remembering that most global negotiations are conducted over dinner.

Antennae up

So, you're great at finance, know marketing inside out, and can talk extensively on supply chain management and the company's masterful strategy. But, in a global organization none of this accounts for a hill of executive beans if you do not have cultural intelligence. The world may feel similar. One international airport is pretty much like another. Big name stores eerily resemble each other whether they are in Nanking or Northampton. But the world is still a very different place wherever you may be. Nanking really isn't Northampton.

Misread the differences and you can cost your organization a lot of money. It might even cost you your job. General Foods squandered millions of dollars trying to introduce Japanese consumers to packaged cake mixes. The company failed to note that only 3 percent of Japanese homes were equipped with ovens. Then, it promoted the idea of baking cakes in Japanese rice cookers. This overlooked the fact that the Japanese use their rice cookers throughout the day to keep rice warm and ready.

Similarly, Philips began to earn a profit in Japan only after it had reduced the size of its coffeemakers to fit in the smaller Japanese kitchens and its shavers to fit in the smaller Japanese hands.

There are a host of other such examples. Some are comical. All are expensive. And all emerge from managers making decisions with their cultural antennae switched off (presuming they have such antennae in the first place).

Decoding culture

What we have observed is that high performing leaders have developed sophisticated skills of cultural decoding. They tap into local cultures because they recognize—among other things— that culture molds who they are and how they see the world. As they want to understand themselves better and see the world in new ways they are culturally open.

Cultural decoding requires the individual

- To have interacted with many cultures and for them to enjoy— and show they enjoy—that interaction.
- To be sensitive to symbols, language, arts, so that they can actively show their appreciation of local context and through their understanding of symbols, art, and history explain that local culture to different audiences. Be careful when criticizing. Know the difference between criticism and thoughtful critique.
- To have experienced an all round education—with a wide variety of degree backgrounds, which may have little directly to do with the role they hold.
- Often to have experienced foreign education somewhere in their early/mid-adulthood.

In addition, we have seen high performing leaders actively develop the skill for decoding cultural cues. This means they have evolved the emotional intelligence to recognize the cue that requires decoding in the first place.

To emphasize further the education and intellectual side to our argument, many of the outstanding leaders we meet have read and continue to read history and can read through history how particular cultures have been shaped and formed. As part of that broader education, leaders, especially the older outstanding leaders, have a broad exposure to religion, philosophy, and art. What is noticeable among many younger, up-and-coming leaders is that they lack both the language and insight into art, philosophy, and religion and can unwittingly come over as overly functionalist—and too much driven by narrow Anglo-American values.

We believe in the future; business schools will need to add to their burgeoning corporate social responsibility (CSR) and ethics courses, by teaching philosophy, religion, and cultural history. Helping students understand how art is appreciated in different parts of the world, for example, could be an important aspect of the business school curriculum—and an essential skill for the next generation of global leaders. (This is already happening. Witness IE Business School's (Madrid) purchase of Segovia University so that business can be combined with other disciplines.)

What is culture?

So, to succeed on the global business stage requires personal cultural intelligence and the ability to operate in a variety of situations over a career. Traditionally, managers have obtained this experience through cross-functional assignments within a company, diverse work teams, or foreign postings. But however they acquire it, it is clear that they require it. Cultural intelligence is a set of behaviors, attitudes, and policies, which enable business leaders and those they lead to work effectively in cross-cultural situations. Without cultural intelligence, they will have no antennae to raise.

Cultural understanding involves respect for history and tradition, and being secure in one's own culture in order to understand others at a deeper level. Think of Tugatu sending 18 people to the United States to explore the meaning of a luxury car as preparation for Toyota's development of the Lexus brand. Perhaps Toyota should look to their past in dealing with their quality problems of today.

These cultural competencies apply at the levels of the individual, the work group, and the organization. They matter whether you are dealing with customers and suppliers, conducting negotiations, or staffing joint ventures. At a personal level, the global manager must possess vision, self-awareness, a tolerance for ambiguity, respect for others, flexibility, resourcefulness, cultural consciousness, and leadership.

This is a demanding list. To better understand it, let's rewind slightly to look at what we actually mean by the word culture.

After uncovering 156 definitions, in their formidable book *Culture: A Critical Review of Concepts and Definitions*, A. L. Kroeber and Clyde Kluckhohn conclude: "Culture consists of patterned ways of thinking, feeling and reacting, acquired and transmitted mainly by symbols, constituting the distinctive achievements of human groups, including their embodiment in artifacts; the essential core of culture consists of traditional (i.e. historically derived and selected) ideas and especially their attached values."[1]

Ed Schein, the MIT professor who first drew attention to the notion of organizational culture, defines it on three levels: first, the upper *visible* level of artifacts and symbols; second, an underlying level of attitudes and normative behavior; and, third, a deeper level of fundamental beliefs and assumptions about the world and purpose of human existence. Understanding this deeper level of culture requires appreciation of the formative context and the history of place and people. Extrapolating culture on societal level shows that the values and assumptions underlying visible culture will continue as deep undercurrents in spite of the extent of changes taking place on the surface. For example, although a visitor to Russia or China can observe signs of Western culture, the older cultural norms still hold sway just below the surface.

It is only through an appreciation of those older norms that one can make sense of modern Russia or China.

The starting point for appreciating another culture is an appreciation of your own. Many of the elements of our upbringing that we take for granted, or assume are universal or enlightened, are rooted in our cultural context. What we think of as knowledge is often something narrower—cultural knowledge. Think of education. Understanding one's educational attainment, ways of learning, management and teaching method and cultural values are just basics—these represent culture-specific knowledge.

Global leaders need to be aware that they themselves carry their own cultural influences with them and need to have the cultural intelligence (CQ) to adapt and develop new behaviors[2] in different multicultural settings.[3]

This cultural baggage is manifest in

Language—communication is the most important skill of a global leader and language is the most important tool.

Personal relationships—forging new relationships and maintaining existing relationships is the central task of the global leader. In particular, a lot of their time is spent on "warming up" and "neutralizing" people who can potentially create problems.

Corporate cultural attaches

When it comes to understanding national cultures, two Dutchmen have led the way in providing a business perspective—Geert Hofstede and Fons Trompenaars.

In Hofstede's hands, culture becomes the crux of business. He defines it as "the collective programming of the mind, which distinguishes the members of one group or category of people from another."[4] Hofstede's conclusions are based on extensive research. His seminal work on cross-cultural management, *Culture's Consequences*, involved a survey of over 100,000 IBM employees from more than 60 countries.

Hofstede identified five basic characteristics that distinguish national cultures. These dimensions are as follows:

Power distance: the extent to which the less powerful members of institutions and organizations expect and accept that power is unequally distributed.

Individualism: the strength of ties between individuals, ranging from loose in some societies to involving greater collectivism and strong cohesive groups in others.

Masculinity: the markedness of the distinction between social gender roles.

Uncertainty avoidance: the extent to which society members feel threatened by uncertain or unknown situations.

Long-term orientation: the extent to which a society exhibits a pragmatic, future-oriented perspective.

More recently, Fons Trompenaars has put his original stamp on notions of culture and how they affect people at work (most notably in his book, *Riding the Waves of Culture*). Trompenaars contends that "culture is a series of rules and methods that a society has evolved to deal with the recurring problems it faces. They have become so basic that, like breathing, we no longer think about how we approach or resolve them. Every country and every organization faces dilemmas in relationships with people, dilemmas in relationship to time, and dilemmas in relationships between people and the natural environment. Mix and match people from different cultures, who interpret such issues diversely, and you have organizational chaos that has to be managed differently than other organization issues."[5]

There is a lot of cultural and organizational chaos around. "Cultural mixing is an everyday feature of organizational life, especially in these times of huge corporate acquisitions, mergers, and alliances. Relational aspects like cultural differences and lack of trust are responsible for 70 per cent of alliance failures," Trompenaars says. "This is even more striking when we realize that building trust is a cultural challenge in itself. Lack of trust is often caused by different views of what constitutes a trustworthy partner. In addition, intercultural alliances involve differences in corporate cultures as well as national cultures.

Perceptions of these, as well as of more-or-less 'objective' cultural variations, can lead to big problems."[6]

Fons Trompenaars' research over almost two decades—involving thousands of employees in more than 50 countries—makes him a leading expert on cultural differences. His work indicates the existence of four broad types of culture, giving rise to four styles of management:[7]

The Family model: This is typical of cultures as seemingly disparate as France, Italy, Japan, and India. The result is a power-oriented corporate culture in which the leader is regarded as the caring head of the family who best knows what should be done and what is good for subordinates.

The Eiffel Tower model: Typified by German companies where authority stems from the occupancy of a given role with prescribed decision-making powers and areas of accountability. Each level in the hierarchy has a clear and demonstrable function of holding together the levels beneath it. Subordinates obey not because of emotional ties reminiscent of a family but because it is their role to obey the person immediately above them.

The Guided Missile model: Is so called because it is based on a view of the organization as a missile homing in on strategic objectives and targets. British companies as well as many American and Swedish companies are typical of this type of organization. The culture is oriented toward tasks and objectives, usually undertaken by teams or project groups. Roles are not fixed. The overriding principle is to do whatever it takes to complete a task or reach a goal.

Incubator model: Typified by the companies of California's Silicon Valley, structured around the fulfillment of the individual members' needs and aspirations. The management framework exists to free individuals from routine tasks so they can pursue creative activities. The only legitimate management function is to protect and enrich the efforts of individuals.

It is where these four sets of cultural assumptions play against each other, says Trompenaars, that things can go wrong. Where problems occur it is often because the decision-making style or formula used does not take account of the different cultural values.

Putting a brake on culture

Terry Brake, author of *The Global Leader*, is another who has researched the impact of cultural differences on business. He notes that contact among cultures is of more than anthropological interest. "A clash of cultures affects the bottom line directly and can destroy a potentially rewarding joint venture or strategic alliance."[8]

The business press is full of stories in which highly successful companies have suddenly become grounded on the hidden sand banks of international cultural differences. As Brake points out: "On paper, Corning's joint venture with the Mexican glass manufacturer Vitro seemed made in heaven. Twenty-five months after it began, the marriage was over. Cultural clashes had eroded the potentially lucrative relationship." What happened? American managers were continually frustrated by what they saw as the slowness of Mexican decision-making. Compared with the United States, Mexico is a hierarchical culture and only top managers make important decisions. Loyalty to these managers is a very high priority in Mexico, and to try to work around them is definitely taboo. The less urgent Mexican approach to time made scheduling very difficult. The Mexicans thought the Americans wanted to move too fast, and vice versa. Communication was also problematic, and not simply because of language.

"American directness clashed with the indirectness of the Mexicans. The Americans often thought that the Mexican politeness was an attempt to hide problems and faults. Corning also thought Vitro's sales style was unaggressive. Over time, the differences were felt to be unbridgeable."

Corning's experience is by no means unique. Disney's experience in France is another high-visibility example. EuroDisney was referred to in British and French newspapers as Corporate America's cultural Vietnam or Chernobyl.

In another case, the sportswear manufacturer Nike withdrew a line of sports shoes. The original design included a motif, which resembled the symbol for Allah, and was deemed disrespectful to people in the Arab world, especially since the shoes would inevitably become dirty. Clearly, the designers at Nike could have made an earlier decision to remove the offending emblem had they had a better understanding of that culture.

Procter & Gamble had a rocky start in Japan, too. Its decision to use an aggressive style of TV advertising (which knocked the competition) offended the Japanese taste for surface harmony, or *wa,* and damaged P&G's initial credibility.

The moment

We could go on. Truth be told, anthropologists and a host of other academics and thinkers have been wrestling with what constitutes culture for centuries. But, to the Indian business executive negotiating a deal in Bucharest, Romania, the variations in definitions are unimportant. What matters is the moment.

So, for the purposes of those doing business, culture can be understood as something which is collective, inherited, learned, valued, and stable while open to evolution. Culture can be seen in visible things—symbols (words, gestures, pictures, or objects that carry a particular meaning which is only recognized by those who share a particular culture); heroes (past or present, real or fictitious persons, who possess characteristics that are highly prized); and rituals (collective activities, often superfluous in reaching desired objectives, but which are socially essential) and in the intangible world of values—broad tendencies for preferences of a certain state of affairs to others (good-evil, right-wrong, natural-unnatural).

National culture is sometimes seen as homogenous, but what's interesting in our experience is how heterogeneous it really is. As we travel around the world, we have observed a hierarchy of culture: organization; then location; and only then national culture.

So an IBM office in Munich will be most influenced by the IBM culture, then the Bavarian influence of the Munich area; and finally the German national culture.

Culture is deeply rooted in the people's history and often shaped by religion and language. Culture resists being captured and easily defined, measured and packed into convenient dimensions. Rather than being a barrier to communication, culture may be better understood as a medium for or context of communication. In our experience, that is how the most effective global leaders think of it. They also appreciate that stereotypes only get you so far.

The global paradox

As well as being problematical to define, culture is also a broad brush. It enables us to *generally*—perhaps tentatively—understand the social morés of a particular society or group of people. This is useful but not enough. Visit China and you will find communal cultures, a large number of different communities each with their own local cultures, but a limited sense of a Chinese national culture. The same phenomenon can be encountered around the world. Cultures aren't uniform—far from it.

The world is more heterogeneous than the rash of global brand names across cityscapes suggest. Consumption patterns may be coalescing, but that does not mean that individuals are any more alike now than they were a century ago. Just because we wear the same jeans, eat at the same fast food restaurants, drive the same cars, and even wear the same designer spectacles does not make us see the world in the same way.

What does this mean for practicing business leaders? This uncomfortable reality has two implications. First, only those with the curiosity to go beyond cultural generalizations will thrive. Second, a key ingredient of this is the ability to sense different situations.

Cultural irritants

Regardless of experiences, global leaders will be challenged by local cultures. Indeed, the day they cease to be challenged is probably the day they stop being culturally sensitive. Global leaders require all their abilities and diplomacy to overcome the cultural obstacles they encounter. There is need for understanding what is valued in each social grouping.

Consider the notion of leadership, for example, which varies from place to place. Depending on your point of view, here are just some of the potential sources of cultural irritation or exultation:[9]

Sweden: Sweden is a consensual, egalitarian, and high-tech society, where leaders are mild-mannered and antithetical to the Anglo-American model of leadership (larger than life, in control, strong, tough, heroic, materialistic, flamboyant). Even so, there is an ongoing convergence toward the Anglo-American model. The materialistic drive to get to the apex of organization is less pronounced in Sweden. The process is slower with an emphasis on experiencing different roles. There is less distance between different hierarchical levels. Showing off is not tolerated and having a flamboyant life style is frowned upon—in 1982, we learned that Stockholm had 1.3 million inhabitants and only 4 Rolls Royce cars.[10] Consensus among leadership teams is a way forward. But, in an ever more highly competitive world, that is changing with an ever growing number of strong leaders ready to take charge.

Israel: In Israel, the idea of leadership is linked with a sense of national destiny and preservation. The military looms large in people's lives. Military service is mandatory for men (three years) and women (two years). Not serving in the military in Israel is like not having a driving license in the United States or United Kingdom—it is frowned upon. Three-quarters of marriages can be traced back to meeting through military service.[11]

Leadership is seen as an oral and interpersonal phenomenon (i.e. fast moving communication). Leaders do not come from elitist background (although a social elite does exist). Leadership is not as much about character but about performing in the moment, perseverance, and personal strength. A high value is placed on improvisation.

France: Leadership is cerebral. The leader must be intelligent with a good education. Being street smart is not highly regarded. For example, if a new CEO is brought in, his first task will be to lock himself in the office and study company documents, analyzing and rationalizing them for months, before proposing a way forward. If a leader is not intellectually stimulating, he is not respected.

French senior executives are required to work with government much more than in other countries. Leaders are typically drawn from the French elite *Grandes Ecoles*—politicians, government officials, and business leaders tend to have the same background, particularly in terms of education. There is less need for leadership as executives can pull rank, relying on hierarchy or social standing. The outstanding leader does not attract too much publicity unlike the Anglo-American model. Intellect must stand out, not personality.

For this reason President Nicolas Sarkozy has frequently been given a bad press. Instead of intellectualizing over his strategy, in the early days of his presidency he severed connections with his wife and began a relationship with a glamorous younger model who speedily became his new wife. There was none of the calculated aloofness of his predecessors. Among the critics of his so-called bling-bling presidency is Laurent Joffrin of *Libération.* "He's perfectly integrated the oh-so- contemporary culture of reality TV made up of exposing the intimate, of popular speech, and of ferocious competition. The soap opera of his love life displayed on glossy pages is just an illustration of that," Joffrin has lamented of Sarkozy.[12]

This was really brought home to us recently when we heard about a French executive who had adopted an American leadership style. In talking about the way forward for the company he used the U.S. style leadership levers of personality and charisma. As the "all seeing leader" he tried to reassure his people that he knew how they felt and what was best for them. In doing so, however, he lost the respect of his French colleagues who wanted to admire his intellectual not his emotional reach.

Another French executive in a different company used a leadership style that resonated with his fellow countrymen and women. First, he demonstrated his keen intellect by a skilful analysis of the situation facing the company—including its competitive advantages and weaknesses. Then he opened the intellectual debate up to his colleagues by asking them what they thought. In this way, he sold the strategy to them because they were encouraged to see it as an intellectual challenge.

Both these companies are in high value sectors—smart businesses—so that does not explain the different reaction. It does show that just as you can stumble into an unfamiliar culture and get it badly wrong, you can also be born into that culture and still make a mess of it. Outsiders do not have the monopoly on cultural faux pas!

This points to an important cultural difference between French and American leadership. Take the first 100 days of a leader's term in office. In France, as indicated earlier, the first 100 days are spent thinking, reflecting, and analyzing all the data. This is the opposite of the Anglo-Saxon view that says you have to hit the ground running.

Russia: Mapping Russian cultural terrain is a hazardous exercise. But Russian corporate culture is often referred to as the Soviet mind-set. That implies a revival of Russian-ness in social and business life and the emergence of the new pattern of behavior in response to the cataclysmic changes of the past 15 years.

The Soviet management style and practices place a high value on cautiousness, predictability, periods of intensive work and rest, and a propensity for working communally. All of these aspects have been conditioned by adversity, crisis, and uncertainty—in this regard, they are not unlike the American frontier experience. But these traditional preferences are now giving way to a new set of behaviors, including risk-taking and entrepreneurial dynamism. However, some things do not change. The Russians still look to a top man, also increasingly the top woman, to take the decision. As one Russian oligarch commented to us, "Russians need to be suppressed. Tsardom is alive and well."

The spiritual level

In addition to national cultures, of course, there are religious cultures, which have to be considered. Knowledge of and respect for different religions is a critical factor in succeeding anywhere in the world.

In the Jewish tradition there is the Talmudic principle—*lifnim mi-shurat ha-din*—which can be translated as "beyond the requirements of the law." This is a positive ethical obligation to exceed the letter of the law, particularly in helping those in difficult economic circumstances.

In Judaism, employer and employee have mutual obligations and rights. Employers must promptly pay wages (refusal to pay is a form of oppression and fraud); and employees owe their employers an honest and full day's work. Both the employer and the community have an obligation to preserve workers' dignity and self-respect.

In Islam, the culture of the mandatory levy—*zakat*—is strong often set at 2.5 percent by the state on savings and assets. Charging of interest—usury or *riba* (the Islamic term)—and speculation are seen as "bad." Interest is replaced by *mudarabah* (profit-sharing under economic cooperation); *musharakah* (equity participation); and their derivatives *murabaha* (cost-plus pricing) including foreign trade and rental.

Only the curious thrive

Let's be clear, we're not saying you have to understand every cultural nuance before you leave home, but you do need to open your mind to alternative ways of thinking. Global leaders don't need to be cultural experts but they do need to show respect for local rituals and ways. A willingness to enter into local customs shows trust and begets trust.

Can we trust you? As Andrew drank his rice wine in Hunan he had little idea of the cultural issues surrounding the rite of passage. This is common. You may not have an idea of the local context. But, the important thing is that you don't challenge it.

What were Andrew's hosts thinking as they poured him the rice wine? Simple: are you honorable, can we trust you? If you are not afraid to get drunk with us we can trust you—because clearly you are putting your trust in them.

So what is the intellectual understanding here? This ritual (and remember it is a regional one that applies in Hunan but not so much in Beijing) is necessary to achieve the purpose for which we are here. We have come to do business—but before we can achieve that goal we have to first have a drink. In another culture, the logic might be the other way round. So, for example, in New York City, it is typical to conduct the business first and then if it goes well, we might go for a drink or have some dinner. Think about it. Both make sense in their respective cultures.

As Andrew drank his twenty-first shot, the minister announced that he considered him a real man and one who could have as many women as he wanted.

There is, of course, a danger that you could be duped. Our experience is that going along with your host's suggestions and behavior is very powerful—and, in the vast majority of cases, safer. Run with it, offend no one, and show that you're willing to work with them on their terms. It's almost like an animal that exposes itself, and every other animal backs off. You have shown such trust in them they cannot progress until they now trust you.

It is also worth remembering that the cultural challenges often apply to local people as well. As Andrew drank the rice wine, the hotel owner and his three sons joined him. One of the sons collapsed early on in the proceedings. Would he be the one likely to inherit the hotel? We doubt it. Cultural tests can be unforgiving—even if you know and understand them.

Situation sensing

The best global leaders have a nose for local cultures and customs. They can sniff out local customs.

"If context is critical, being sensitive to that context, being able to detect the way the wind is blowing, is essential for any leader.

Authentic leaders have good, sometimes excellent, situation-sensing capabilities," say Rob Goffee and Gareth Jones in their book *Why Should Anyone Be Led By You?*[13]

Goffee and Jones believe there are three separate, but related, elements to effective situation-sensing. The first is made up of observational and cognitive skills. "Leaders see and sense what's going on in their organizations—and then use their cognitive skills to interpret these observations. They pick up and interpret soft data sometimes without any verbal explanation. They know when team morale is shaky or when complacency needs challenging. They collect information, seemingly through osmosis, and use it to understand the context in which they are aspiring to lead," Goffee and Jones write.

The second element of situation-sensing is made up of behavioral and adaptive skills. Having observed and understood the situation, effective leaders adjust their behaviors. They adapt without ever losing their sense of self. They are, what Goffee and Jones call, *authentic chameleons.*

The final element of effective situation-sensing is that leaders use their own behavior to change the situation. They exemplify an alternative context. Goffee and Jones point to the example of Mayor Rudy Gulianni of New York in the aftermath of 9/11 as an example. He sensed the need for highly visible leadership and went to what in the days that followed became Ground Zero. By articulating the shock and grief of New Yorkers, but also their pride in the courage of their emergency services, and by exemplifying their gritty resolve, he began the process of recovery.

No excuses

As a final point, it is worth noting that culture is routinely given as an excuse. We Japanese do not do things like you Americans. We Brits do not do things like this. Reluctance to change should be distrusted. Culture is usually not the reason why something shouldn't happen.

Ask Yourself

- What do you know about the culture of your organization?
- When you go to another country, what do you prepare for—the meeting or the cultural exchange?
- How much time do you spend understanding the local context and culture?
- Do you actually respect other cultures?
- How do you develop and refine your cultural antennae?
- Does your cultural curiosity go beyond dinner table conversation?

Learn the language of business

Words have alternative meanings depending on where you are in the world. Handle with care.

Lost in translation

Language is increasingly important. In one global organization based in France, it was decreed that the company's language should be English. When a group of French managers chose to have a meeting in French the highest ranked was fired for breaking the corporate code.

Language can be a bonding force or one which simply highlights disunity. The reality is that companies speak different languages. Corporate languages are shaped by their cultures as much as decrees as to which language should be spoken. Even though they may share the same official language, meanings differ from one corporation to the next.

This means that the room for confusion and misunderstanding is immense. Global advertising and branding show us how easily cultural problems relating to language can be overlooked.

Getting to snow

Just how stubbornly resistant to reality cultural misconceptions and myths can be, once they take root, is clear from the misunderstandings that arise from the use and abuse of language.

Take snow, for example. In 1940, linguist, Benjamin Lee Whorf, claimed that while English has only one word for snow, Eskimo has many, with separate words for falling snow, slushy snow, and so on.

However, the amateur linguist had misinterpreted some 1911 research of Eskimo languages. Whorf's article contained two major errors. First, English has several words for snow, including powder, sleet, and slush. Second, comparing word-counts between radically different languages has little meaning.[14]

The Inuits (the modern term for Eskimo) make extensive use of prefixes and suffixes, combining several concepts into a long, compound word. English-speakers can say the same thing by using several words instead of one long one. For example, in Inuktitut (an Inuit language), the generic term for snow is "aput." In English we add an adjective to describe the concept of "new snow." Inuktitut expresses the same concept by adding suffixes to make the single word "aputiqarniq."

Whorf's observation that Inuits use many words for snow was misleading. But it became widely accepted. Some reports put the number at 50, or 100, or even 200 words. The linguists at Canada's Department of Indian and Northern Affairs now report "over 30" variations of Inuktitut words for snow, all of them based on just a few root words.

While there may not be 400 words in Inuit for "snow," the globalization of business means that there is plenty of scope for confusion over language and its meaning.

In German, it is said that there are 18 variations to middle management. In Russian, there are very few alternatives to "father Czar." Similarly, the word efficiency does not exist in Russian, is intermixed with effectiveness in French, and, of course, dominates Anglo-American discourse. The word privacy has similar cultural dissonances as we shall see.

In Arabic, leadership does not have an exact synonym based on the conceptualization in the West. Leadership is *Al Kiyada* or *Al Zaam'*. This Arabic translation of leadership means "command and control" similar to the military concept of leadership. However, one cannot understand leadership in the Arab world if one removes it from its Islamic context. Islamic leadership is conceptualized as *sayyisd al qawmi khadimuhu*m meaning that "leaders are servants of the followers." As such it closely relates to the Western concept of servant-leadership. It is interesting that the literal translation of command and control when contextualized in the Arabic world refers to servant-leadership. Take nothing literally; always contextualize.

Universal language

Perhaps the obvious solution to language confusion is just to have a single language. It would save money too.

The European Union is home to roughly 500 million Europeans, with a diverse ethnic and cultural background. Understandably they speak many different languages—27 member states and 23 official languages. Plus there are more than 60 indigenous regional or minority languages, from ancient Celtic languages like Welsh to minority tongues such as Kashubian in Poland.

In the spirit of diversity, the EU accords equal status to its official languages, allowing each member state to address the EU in its mother tongue. Furthermore, the EU insists that countries seeking accession to the EU protect minority language rights. Good news for speakers of minority languages, such as Romany and Ruthenian, who fear for the survival of their language.

But all this language goodwill comes at a significant cost. Protecting linguistic diversity meant that, in 2009, the EU employed 1,750 translators working full time on translating documents and on other language-related activities, together with some 600 support staff.

In an effort to reduce costs, only meetings of EU leaders and ministers are translated into all official languages. Lower-level meetings are translated into a few of the major languages. Translation on this scale is still expensive, however. In 2008 the EU translated 1,805,689 pages of material. The year before, with fewer pages translated, the translation budget was one billion euros.

Diversity of language is an admirable objective. The reality is though that one language usually dominates business proceedings. History tells us that languages rise and fall with empires. In the days of the Roman Empire the international language of business was Latin. Before that it was Greek. After the fall of the Roman Empire, several languages competed for influence. For many years French was the language of the nobility and diplomacy.

The extent of the British Empire, and then the United States and its sphere of economic influence, means that English has been the dominant business language of the past century. Yet, as globalization continues apace, and Western economic hegemony is eroded are we right to assume that English will remain the international business language?

English may be the lingua franca of international business in 2009 (1,308,700 pages of the total 1,805,689 pages translated in the EU were produced in English), but what about the billion or so Mandarin speakers in China, the world's fastest growing superpower. Consider the third of a billion plus Spanish speakers scattered across the globe, or the 200 million or so Arabic speakers.

There have been attempts in the past to ease the world's communication problems by creating a language that would be acceptable to all nations. To date, however, such efforts have failed.

In 1887, Ludovic Zamenhof published details of a new language using the pseudonym Doktoro Esperanto. It was a laudable attempt to reduce conflict between neighboring communities of Poles, Russians, and Germans. Esperanto, as the language became known, was later described by the U.S. government as a "neutral interlanguage … not identifiable with any alliance or ideology" and "far easier to learn and use than any national language."

Despite its obvious qualifications, Esperanto never became a universal language. Ultimately, as remains the case today, nationalism prevailed. For example, a move to have the language adopted by the League of Nations was blocked by France, who subsequently banned the language from its schools. Josef Stalin called it "that dangerous language." Governments across

Central Europe obstructed use of the language. Esperanto speakers were persecuted in some countries and even shot.

Understanding context

Not every language faux pas is as obvious as the many slogan slip ups. Some language issues are far more subtle. That's why clever chairmen or chief executives devote time to understanding meaning in a local context. They sit down and say, "What does respect mean over here, and is it going to influence our brand?" "What does pricing mean?" So, the first challenge must always be to understand the context.

This requires that you ask very basic questions. This is particularly contentious if you have a global product, and even more so if you are in the pharmaceutical industry. What does pricing mean in Africa? Pricing, in certain African countries, if we're dealing with an AIDS-related product or issue, actually means making a loss. This needs to be fully explored. A financial loss in one market is not necessarily a loss overall. Can you get support from the WHO? Can you get support from the UN? What are the related PR and brand development possibilities?

Doing business globally and exploring the language issues leads you to unlikely and profound discussions. It gets to the essence of what business is and hopes to achieve. But, as a leader, can you imagine taking time out of your busy calendar to sit in Namibia or elsewhere for two days talking about things that you initially feel are irrelevant?

If the first issue is context, the second challenge is to develop a lexicon for your working group, company, community, team or however you define it. "There's a common language that comes through discussing," one leader told us. "But, if you simply try to have your own way, then it's not fair, it's not good for the shareholders. In this kind of climate, if you are overly assertive with the board of directors and at the same time with the executive managers of the company, then many feel that there is a problem between the chairman and CEO and they rapidly lose confidence."

At Nestlé, for example, major changes in the company were championed under the banner "Renovate and innovate." At P&G its new approach to research and development was encapsulated in the call to "connect and develop." Such phrases act as a powerful shorthand to communicate complex and compelling messages. They are the soundbites of the corporate world, which for the unsuspecting need to be decoded.

Ask Yourself

- Do you make the time to key into local contexts and local meanings?
- How do you ensure there is a shared language in your team, division or organization?
- What are the key messages you are communicating? Are they compelling?
- Are you sure that these key messages are understood?

Master meetings that matter

In the Anglo-American world, a meeting is held in a formal space for a specific purpose—to discuss x or y. But in places such as Turkey, people meet in a restaurant without having a designated aim—and do business. Which kind of meeting is it?

Meeting of the minds

Meetings are at the heart of business. For some they are a necessary evil, for others a fundamental part of getting deals done. Meetings come in various types: formal and informal. In some countries, such as the United Kingdom for example, there are even laws governing the conduct of specific types of meetings.

Not all cultures regard meetings in the same light either. Some see meetings as an opportunity to accomplish business activities, and are concerned about the effectiveness and productivity of meetings. But in other countries meetings are more about relationship building than getting things done.

What is not in dispute is that, like many other aspects of doing business, meetings are a cultural minefield, providing countless opportunities for causing inadvertent offence.

Tempus fugit

Timing is everything in business. Western executives, in particular, are obsessed with it; after all, time is money. Each and every move is mapped out in personal organizers. Diaries are divided into half hour segments, 15 minutes even. They rush from meeting to meeting, pausing only to read *The One Minute Manager* on the plane.

The trouble is that though time is universal, our attitudes to time differ wildly. One executive's nine o'clock prompt is another's "around half past nine if I can make it."

As in so many other areas, national stereotypes abound, with some degree of justification if anecdotal evidence is to be believed. Germans are sticklers for punctuality, as are the Swiss. Indeed, it is no coincidence that Switzerland is renowned for the quality of its watches. If they say a nine o'clock start for a business meeting in Switzerland, do not arrive a minute later. Whereas in some Mediterranean countries people are accustomed to lateness or even of nonarrival. In one breath, they complain, "why is he/she keeping me waiting" and yet in the next, "that's him/her." All around laugh and continue what they are doing. Why worry about time?

Attitudes to time keeping can be regarded as local customs. "To some extent national stereotypes do fit," says one international businessman, who lives on the France-Switzerland border. "In Germany or Switzerland you do not turn up 15 minutes late to a meeting, while in France that would be quite acceptable. Things are changing. With business becoming more global, larger companies do tend to put greater emphasis on punctuality. In smaller French companies, however, attitudes are much more casual."

In Germany, Switzerland, and Scandinavia punctuality is expected. A few minutes late and you can wave goodbye to the lucrative contract. Lateness is strictly for amateurs and who wants to do business with them? Mark McCormack, the founder and chairman of International Management Group, and a serious and unremitting globetrotter, once remarked of traveling to Geneva: "Here, more than anywhere else on earth, be on time."

The British approach to punctuality is less predictable. Renowned for fastidious good manners and emotional caution, the British are surprisingly casual about timekeeping; ironic for a nation that numbers a clock, Big Ben, among its landmarks.

"I've been to many meetings in the UK and found that when I've arrived I have been the only one there," admits one bemused executive. "The others eventually arrive with various excuses. It's strange when you consider that meetings are the most important management activity in the UK—they are where the work gets done. Contrast that with Italy where meetings are for posturing and eloquence and the real work gets done later."

When it comes to timekeeping, the Italians remain a glorious law unto themselves. "For Italians punctuality is simply not in their culture," says one regular business visitor to Italy. "They live for the moment. If you agree to meet at 12 o'clock and your Italian colleagues arrive half an hour late, they will invariably not have an excuse but a great idea. They'd be affronted if you didn't celebrate with them. The fact that you've been sitting there is irrelevant." One cynical executive observes that the British pretend to be German but would, in fact, love to be Italian.

In Spain straightforward honesty overcomes a less than Germanic adherence to punctuality—if they are going to be an hour late, Spanish executives will quickly inform you of the fact. It can't be helped.

Once outside Europe, punctuality becomes ever more complex. Europeans would generally accept that time is money and, therefore, a valuable commodity. A few minutes doesn't really make much difference, even if it may be slightly annoying or mystifying at the time. But, what if time isn't money? It isn't in Japan, where it is more important to make the right decision. The Japanese arrive well prepared and on time, because they want to make sure that they make the best possible decision for their business. And, that can take some time.

Indeed the Peruvian government was so concerned about tardiness that it launched a national punctuality campaign called "la hora sin demora," or "time without delay." The idea was to abolish the country's relaxed approach to timekeeping—La Hora Peruana (Peruvian time)—which tolerated people arriving anything up to an hour late to an appointment.[15]

Pleased to meet you

In the event that a meeting should actually take place, the next cultural hurdle to overcome is how to introduce yourself.

Today, in almost every country around the world the common rule in business is to shake hands on meeting and leaving. In a group, you should shake hands with everyone present. Keep handshakes gentle. Few people are impressed by having their knuckles crushed.

Those tempted to dismiss such formalities might consider that the reasons for shaking hands go beyond good manners. The handshake is a symbolic offering of the hand of friendship. Psychologists have also found that appropriate tactile contact is an acceptable way to move into another person's personal space, and can help break down barriers.

The onus here is on what is culturally appropriate. It is unlikely that men will have to experience a kiss from other men. Even when this is common practice, in Russia for example, it is usually reserved for friends. Similarly, women generally kiss only other women who are friends. Male to female kisses in a business context, even among close associates, should be brief and chaste.

In Asia, a handshake may be preceded by a brief bow from the waist. In some Asian countries the degree of politeness offered may depend on the status of the visitor.

Using the appropriate level of familiarity with names is also important. Though globalization means that many countries are adopting the informal business practices of the Anglo-Saxon world, travelers can still find themselves caught out by the cultural minefield of forms of address. The general rule is to be formal until invited to do otherwise. In Europe outside the United Kingdom (and even there often) early use of first names is seen as overfamiliarity and is frowned on. (Likewise, do not use familiar forms of the second person singular—*tu* and *du* in French and German, for example—until the other person suggests you might like to.)

Names are, of course, a potential source of trouble for innocents abroad. Most people are probably aware that Chinese names come in the opposite order to those in the West, with the family name first followed by the given name (sometimes with a middle name in between). Hence Wu Jichuan is Mr Wu. (But watch out for "Westernized" Chinese names, notably in Taiwan, where a Western first name may precede the Chinese family name.) Names are also in "reverse" order in some other Asian countries such as Thailand and South Korea, though not in Japan, where given names precede family names.

Hispanic cultures frequently use the family names of both father and mother (father's first). Both are used in writing, but generally only the father's in spoken address. In Latin America, people with professional or academic titles such as doctor or professor may prefer to be addressed by those titles alone.

Russian names follow the Western style but the middle name is a "patronymic" derived from the father's given name. For example, Anna Arkadyevna Karenin is Mrs Karenin though it is also respectful to call her Anna Arkadyevna. Note that in Russia women take a feminine form of their husband's name—strictly it is Anna Arkadyevna Karenina but non-Russian speakers can probably ignore this with impunity.

Arabic names are similar, with a middle patronymic denoting son of, *bin*, or daughter of, *bint*. The title *Sheik* is widespread and may denote either a princely ruler or someone versed in the Koran. This title is used in conjunction with the person's given name. Non-titled individuals may be addressed in a variety of ways and it is polite to ask how they wish to be referred to.

Business in the United Kingdom is almost as informal as in the United States with first names used easily and without waiting to be invited. However, a number of leading UK businessmen have received titles as a mark of respect for their business success and this can be a quicksand for foreigners.

The British system of hereditary or bestowed titles deserves a book in itself—indeed there are many such guides. A knight is referred to as Sir plus the given name—"Sir John." His wife is Lady Anne. The female equivalent of a knight (a Dame) is also Lady Anne though sometimes Dame Anne, but her husband is not Sir John. A Lord is referred to as Lord plus family name—Lord McDonald—or assumed or family title—Lord Cranberry. Never "My Lord." Only bow properly or curtsy to royalty.

Card collecting

On any trip make sure you have plenty of business cards. Many cultures expect to exchange cards on first meeting and you may be embarrassed if you don't have any. You may also lose some respect.

Ideally, you should have your business card translated into the local language of wherever you are visiting on one side, again as a mark of respect. The other side should be in your own language.

Take your time. It's impossible to convey respect if you fling your card at someone. In Japan, and some other Asian countries, it is respectful to present your card with both hands, Asian language side up, and hold the card you receive with both as you read.

Don't forget either that in many Asian and Middle Eastern countries the left hand is regarded as "unclean," so avoid giving or receiving business cards with that hand. And take a business card case to keep other people's business cards in.

Make sure you read the other person's card carefully as soon as you are given it, in most Asian countries this is expected as a mark of respect. Place business cards on the meeting room table if there is one, so that you can refer to them during the meeting.

Some cultures regard business cards as an extension of the person's status. Respecting the card shows you respect them. While you may write on your own card, never write on someone else's business card. (And don't write in red ink.)

Are you sitting comfortably?

In many cultures people do not sit randomly in meetings, instead there is a very distinct etiquette. Usually, seating accords with status. Hosts will often be seated in a semi-circle with the highest ranking person sitting just to one side of the center of the semi-circle and the rest of the local executives on the same side. The head of the visiting team will sit to the other side of the center with the rest of the team on that same side.

Even if you are on your own, in a formal business meeting setting it is best to take your seating cue from the host. During the meeting, take notes, don't blow your nose, point or otherwise gesticulate, say "no"—if it can be avoided.

At the conclusion of the meeting, wait for your host to stand up before you do. Say your goodbyes. If it is a first meeting, you may also exchange gifts.

A time and a place

Meeting environments vary depending on country and degree of formality. In Japan, for example, meetings tend to be arranged weeks in advance and take place in formal settings, unlike the informal karaoke entertainment that you may experience after a meeting.

People are creatures of habit. Within organizations employees tend to coalesce around familiar spaces. In the United States and the United Kingdom, for example, the trusty watercooler holds a special place in corporate folklore. Ideas and information are traded at the watercooler: it acts as an informal hub, a meeting place where encounters occur between employees.

Inspired by this interaction organizations have attempted to re-create it on a larger scale. One notable example was Scandinavian Air Systems' (SAS) redesign of its corporate HQ to resemble a street with shops and meeting rooms, in an effort to boost social interaction believing that this would improve business performance. SAS's street concept linked shopping, eating, medical and sports facilities and multirooms with comfortable furniture for meetings, coffee machines, and shared office supplies. These spaces were explicitly designed to create informal interactions.

And at Xerox's Wilson Center for Research and Technology, the organization created the LX Common—a space designed to support informal interaction among groups who normally worked independently. The semi-enclosed space was located at the center of the lab, forcing people to cross through it as they moved in and out of the labs. It contained the kitchen, photocopiers, and printers.

In both cases the results were not quite as intended. At SAS the redesign had little effect, with most interaction still occurring in private offices. While at Xerox although different groups started to use the LX Common to hold meetings, individuals who didn't want to join in or disrupt the meetings were making detours of several hundred feet to avoid walking through the space.

Research by John Weeks, an assistant professor at INSEAD, the international business school based in France, and Anne-Laure Fayard, an assistant professor at Polytechnic University, Brooklyn, New York, revealed that there are three dimensions that governed social interaction at work.

The first is privacy: a soundproof office affords more privacy than a public waiting room, putting people at ease. The second is propinquity: the opportunity to socialize by being in the same place as another person but also in a setting where there is social pressure for face-to-face communication. And finally social designation. Social designation is about the roles and activities that individuals perceive to be appropriate in a given space.

Given that an individual's understanding of each can be shaped by their culture, it is no wonder that intercultural meetings can be complicated affairs.

Shaping board meetings

The way individuals in meetings are also shaped to a degree by the conventions of a particular meeting type and the rules and regulations that may govern that meeting. Board meetings are an obvious example and one where the role of the chairman as a "culture carrier," modeling and determining the behavior of other board members is very important.

So in Germany, for example, board meeting are shaped by the German corporate code, which is intended to promote a culture of open discussion on both the executive and supervisory boards, with the chairman of the supervisory board held responsible for promoting dialog on both boards. Much to the frustration of the Anglo-American mind-set, meetings feel as a dilution of decision-making fluidity. Actually the critical stakeholders are brought into the debate, resulting in cohesive alignment. It takes longer, but the organization is that much stronger.

In a country like Turkey, however, where there is much less governance of board meetings, and a lot more family businesses, the approach is often more open and informal.[16] "In Turkey we do things differently. It's not that we do better than western boards. It's just different. You are brought up with these ground rules and you learn from an early age how to address sensitive issues. It is part of the culture. I think you learn the art of dialogue from the family so when you come to the board it means that others have recognized that you have learned well," one Turkish board member told us.

Members of Turkish boards suffer less from Anglo-American inhibition and are more confident in raising issues sometimes formally, but more often informally. Chairmen of Turkish boards seem able to mitigate the potentially negative consequences of damaging relationships and nurture balanced power structures within the board. Board meetings are held far more frequently than in the United States, for example, often once a week. This informal approach, say Turkish executives, enhances trust and respect.

Ask Yourself

- How much of your time is taken up by meetings?
- How much of your time in meetings is productive?

- How do you measure the success of your meetings?
- What kind of meetings do you run?
- Do you use different locations for different meetings?
- Which of your meetings are the most productive?
- Which different types of meeting have you attended in the last year?
- Which meetings have been most successful in building your business relationships?

Be responsible for business

Corporate responsibility can be confined and defined or be concerned with taking responsibility in society.

To CSR or not to CSR

The purpose of business is a source of continuing debate. This has focused in recent years on corporate social responsibility (CSR). Once the sole preserve of socially progressive companies, now it seems every company is jumping on the CSR bandwagon. But most companies are not embracing CSR for altruistic reasons. Instead firms realize that adopting a CSR agenda offers many benefits.

Some economists, notably Milton Friedman, have argued that social responsibility has no place within the corporation. The role of the corporation, they maintain, is to make profits and deliver value to shareholders. Friedman famously asserted that social responsibility was a "fundamentally subversive doctrine," saying: "There is one and only one social responsibility of business—to use its resources and engage in activities designed to increase its profits."

What these economists overlooked was that a company can focus on its core business, make profits, deliver value to shareholders, and still behave in a socially responsible manner. Russell Sparkes, a director of the UK Social Investment Forum and author of *Socially Responsible Investment—A Global Revolution* defined CSR as the situation when companies are judged "not just by the products and profits they make, but also by how those profits are made." It is not the same as corporate philanthropy.

A number of drivers are involved in the rush to adopt socially responsible business practices.

CSR has an important role in risk management. Companies that have experienced a crisis or been embroiled in a scandal often turn to CSR as part of a risk management program.

Closely allied to risk management is another driver: reputation management. In a brand-conscious world a company must protect the value of its brand.

The drive toward CSR isn't always internal. CSR can be forced upon a corporation by external pressures. Stakeholders, like communities and shareholders, or regulatory bodies, can steer companies toward CSR. Equally, companies hope that by displaying an interest in CSR, however superficial, they will avoid further regulation.

Another important driver is the rise of socially responsible investment (SRI). In the United States, SRI funds account for over $2 trillion worth of investment. With that level of investment interest no company wants to risk the stigma of being removed from the list of acceptable investments.

CSR has even caught on at a national level as governments realize that it could be a useful part of national competitive strategy. To make an impact on national competitiveness, CSR must be adopted at a higher level than simply the corporate. Adopted on an industry-wide basis, or legislative basis, CSR has the potential to boost exports and increase the flow of Foreign Direct Investment—a particularly attractive proposition for developing countries.

While corporations attempt to convince the world of their socially responsible credentials, cynics remain unimpressed. CSR is frequently dismissed as style over substance, a public relations exercise, naked self-interest. No matter how hard some companies try, and how genuinely they take their corporate responsibilities, many commentators remain skeptical. Perhaps a cursory glance at Adam Smith's moral philosophy will silence these doubters, as the father of free market economics emphasized balancing wealth creation with ethical sensibility.[17]

Making a difference

While activists are quick to accuse companies of greenwashing—adopting CSR policies for show rather than through a sense of responsibility—in practice an increasing number of CEOs are deeply committed to CSR activities.

Ben & Jerry's Homemade in the United States, for example, one of the most recognized ice cream brands in the world, and founded by Ben Cohen and Jerry Greenfield in 1978, is famous for its social mission.

Indeed the social mission is so fundamental to Ben & Jerry's core purpose that it was enshrined in the reporting structure when the company was sold to Unilever.

Following that sale the company's activist approach continues to be championed by CEO Walt Freese. Ben & Jerry's engages in a range of socially responsible activities. These activities include making a commitment to sustainable dairy and sustainable agriculture, family farms, fair trade certified and other forms of socially and environmentally sustainable sourcing, reducing its carbon footprint and making progress toward becoming carbon neutral globally, speaking out on behalf of world peace, and supporting the organization Peace One Day.

So, for example, many raw materials are sourced from cooperatively run farmer associations, while the sustainable Caring Dairy initiative promotes sustainable farming at a number of supplier dairy farms, which are benchmarked against sustainability indicators such as animal welfare, biodiversity, and climate impact.

There is no question that socially responsible companies can make a real difference to people's lives. Around the world millions of smallholder farmers eke out an existence—there are 25 million coffee smallholders alone—at the mercy of commodity prices and retailer power. Regrettably, judging by the Doha trade negotiations saga, governments are some way off addressing these issues. Yet consumer power can still make a difference to the terms of world trade, and, in doing so, help alleviate global poverty.

Take the Fairtrade movement. At its most basic, fairtrade is a means of boosting the trading power of small producers from the poorest economies, and doing some social good at the same time. Fairtrade means that farmers get a guaranteed minimum price for their goods covering their costs of sustainable production, plus a premium to invest in the future, so that it benefits the whole community. The extra pricing element that goes toward communal projects is often referred to as the social premium; the amount varies by product, even by region, and with some products, such as coffee, by quality.

Sorting out who's who in the fairtrade world can be confusing. There is IFAT (the International Fairtrade Association) a global network of several hundred fairtrade organizations in more than 70 countries, EFTA (the European Fairtrade Association), NEWS (Network of European Worldshops), and FLO (the Fairtrade Labelling Organization) a group of fairtrade labeling initiatives that operate certification and standards monitoring for fairtrade products.

Fairtrade is not just about a fair price, though. Each organization has its own standards. IFAT has ten fairtrade standards that Fair Trade Organizations (FTOs) receiving the FTO mark must meet. These cover a range of issues including gender equity, working conditions, child labor, and a fair price. The FLO divides standards into four groups: economic, labor, environmental, and social.

The fairtrade universe, then, consists of a number of stakeholders: producers—mostly smallholders, who are organized into associations of some kind, plus a few plantations; 100 percent fairtrade companies; companies that sell some fairtrade products; the Fairtrade Mark—the ISO of the fairtrade world; the consumers; and the campaigners—both organizations, including the pioneering NGO's, as well as individuals.

Measuring good behavior

A Japanese manager we met felt passionately responsible for all parts of his global business. He ensured that he understood the local context for the various manufacturing, marketing, and sales outlets in different parts of the world. To make sure that others also understood, he introduced a cultural audit and a way of thinking about local cultures so that the local managers could integrate local cultural practices with the disciplines required from the corporate center.

Interestingly, having paid attention to how to integrate corporate center requirements into local practices, the firm emerged as being more American than many other Japanese firms. This was largely because of the performance philosophy they had developed, while at the same time being attentive to the teams and people. The corporate center and manufacturing plants in Japan were more American in their practice and orientation than some of the American manufacturing plants in the United States, where the team culture and care and sensitivity for people so predominated that the stakeholder approach had become a way of life.

The Japanese manager talked with all his managers about the critical factors affecting performance—the hard and soft measures concerning motivation. Having communicated that message to each of the regional managers and the country managers, the Japanese manager toured the world making sure that all of his managers, including managers of major plants, understood how they should integrate hard and soft measures of performance measurement.

You cannot manage what you don't measure, and CSR is no exception. Once again cultural antennae need to be raised—as they were by the Japanese manager. Measuring CSR performance does present challenges; universal SR measurement is almost a pointless exercise, environmental metrics are not easily aggregated for the purposes of comparison, country to country, region to region comparisons are often meaningless; and for some areas, such as biodiversity for instance, metrics don't even exist yet.

Cultural Social Responsibility

Corporate Social Responsibility is a controversial concept. On the one hand the impression is that issues such as climate change, water shortage, and environmental pollution have pushed CSR to the top of the corporate agenda. Yet the reality is that there is little agreement over a definition of CSR even within nations, let alone between nations. And there is considerable debate over the extent to which CSR is desirable, or even permissible as a corporate objective.

Given the disparate attitudes toward CSR, a number of nongovernmental organizations, including the International Institute for Sustainable Development, the International Institute for Environment and Development, and the World Conservation Union, have joined forces to contribute to the development of international Social Responsibility standards by the International Organization for Standardization (ISO).

As part of the development process a briefing document was produced outlining the varying attitudes toward CSR in different nations. The document notes that notions of what constitutes a "responsible" organization or enterprise differ between and within countries, depending on historical and cultural factors; social responsibility has certain connotations depending on location; awareness of, interest in, and drivers for engagement with CSR, vary from one country to the next.

So, for example, social responsibility is mainly referred to as "Responsabilidad Social Empresarial," in Chile, a Spanish expression which can be translated as "Entrepreneurial Social Responsibility." In South Africa, corporate social responsibility, sustainable development, corporate citizenship, corporate social investment, and sustainability are popular terms. In the United Kingdom, CSR and corporate responsibility are the usual terms. In Russia, a report by Professor Yuri Blagov of St Petersburg University provides the most comprehensive and integrated perspective drawing together leadership, CSR, and corporate strategy.

In developing countries factors such as poverty, poor governance, and weak civil society means that there are fewer social responsibility drivers. Individuals are more concerned with making a living than improving working conditions, promoting socially responsible products, or reducing carbon output.

Surveys in India frequently report that companies do not see a link between socially responsible practices and financial success. They view social responsibility as a low priority at best, irrelevant at worse.

Agendas and drivers differ across nations. In Chile social responsibility is seen as a voluntary commitment. In South Africa, however, laws relating to black economic empowerment (BEE) and other social issues mean that social responsibility is associated with government legislation and external regulation.

Equally, firms that are involved in social responsibility activities in Chile tend to concentrate on worker conditions, environmental issues, community issues, and social development. In South Africa, black economic empowerment (BEE) and affirmative action are synonymous. In India CSR work related to disaster-affected communities is often a priority.

The CSR challenge

In the Anglo-American world, managers see corporate responsibility in defined areas—legal, for example. But in places such as Russia, it is about taking responsibility in society. The shareholder and stakeholder views appear to be contradictory at best. The one organization that has brought together business, academia, government, and NGOs and shown the way to encompassing shareholder and stakeholder considerations is the European Academy of Business in Society (EABIS). It has become the global forum on how to implement CSR to company and community advantage. EABIS's accomplishment has been to bring together business, academia, third sector, and government and stimulate powerful dialog. No easy matter!

Shareholder value basically deals with those people that have resources who want more value. Stakeholder value takes the majority of people in the organization, not just the elite. So when a Western company goes into China, the basic assumption is that you want to get into a contract which fundamentally looks after the bulk of the people. For one Chinese company that came to Britain, they did much the same—though without the traditional friendly payments. They made sure that the people on the shop floor were well cared for. However, they created a new elite—their own Chinese managers. So if you look at it at both ends, the shared objective is usually to enable stakeholders in the business to earn a decent living wage. It's just done in two different contexts and two different ways, but it's the same principle. And that's the difficulty we have.

Ask Yourself

- How do you integrate long-term sustainability into both the operations and strategy of your business?
- Is CSR something you need to do to do good—corporate benevolence—or is it part of your strategy?
- To what extent do you know how effective your CSR practices are?
- How do you know that your senior and middle managers believe in CSR?
- In reality what messages have an impact on your employees and stakeholders?

Speak up without talking down

Received wisdom says that attitudes toward speaking out are different across countries and this is seen as a cultural issue. For example, the Chinese do not typically speak up. But it isn't so much cultural (national) as company specific. If managers speak up then workers follow their lead. Once you relate it to saving money or doing a better job, people become strident.

Being empowered to speak up in China

In Tianjin is a watch making-factory, Sea-gull, which has received orders from international brands for the manufacture of various watch parts. Interestingly, this factory was actually one of the model communist factories under Mao Tse Tung. Many of the people who work there, either as operatives or as supervisors or as middle managers, were appointed in the old days. Through its original general manager, this particular plant developed a culture of speaking up whenever there were issues that needed to be addressed. These could be performance-related; personality-related; or relationship-related issues concerning teams or relationships between various parts of the organization, such as manufacturing, R&D, and quality control.

So having set up a culture of never fearing to speak up, this philosophy survived from the communist era to the present, more entrepreneurial era. The same managers, the same philosophy, and the same original group are still there making sure that the willingness and courage to speak out continues into the future.

When we visited this factory on one of our visits to China the staff provided examples of concerns that had not been addressed or had not been known about and that lay under the surface concerning the quality of manufacture and quality of R&D to meet international requirements. The women supervisors were determined that all of these quality issues came to the surface, which they did. As a result, they were able to renegotiate their contracts from German, British, French, global brands of high quality in the field of timepieces and time keeping.

Fear of authority

Let's be realistic. The fear of speaking up is widespread in organizations wherever they are in the world.

One project manager described his boss as "the bulldozer who blows nasty commands all the time. [He] destroys meetings when he's there. No one will speak up." Another said she feared being further invalidated by speaking up to her boss, saying, "He has this way of making you feel like an idiot."

More common are reports of loud, aggressive behavior that respondents find frightening and threatening and therefore seek to avoid experiencing. For example, a foreign marketing manager explained why she and other managers believed that speaking up was risky based on the previous responses of the country manager. "He would be very emotional, saying 'it's bullshit' and these kinds of words and raising his voice and getting up and using really dominant behaviour toward the presenter." When you directly witness scenes, said another, where "people are insulted, abused verbally and really shaken," it creates an atmosphere "where it gets more and more difficult to speak up to management." In contrast, those situations described as "totally safe" almost invariably included descriptions of leaders who actively modeled openness and consideration.

People routinely still describe speaking up to authorities as inherently risky. A middle manager in manufacturing explained that such fear exists even when the authority has done little to overtly signal danger in confronting him, "There is a fear of power ... [My boss X, the site head] is a wonderful manager, I think the world of him and he does a great job. But still, I think just the position of manager, or V.P., or any higher power, there's a bit of a fear factor. There's this perception of power and authority, and I think people act differently." A counterpart from another manufacturing facility explained his own fear of speaking up similarly: "It's not human behaviour. I mean, they're senior management. We respect them, but we're going to maintain our appropriate distance, and not come and tell [them] things." Said another, "No one wants to be the one to tell the emperor he doesn't have any clothes on."

Organizational reality is often far removed from the rational ideal in which good ideas surface and foster the continuous questioning, experimenting, and improving needed to thrive in a dynamic world. Silence frequently rules thanks to previous negative experiences with a particular boss, broad social and economic factors that limit employee mobility, and an evolutionary heritage that triggers an automatic fear reaction in even seemingly benign settings. Whatever the reason, there are immense human and organizational costs to silence. These costs range from lost opportunities for productive dialog about technical or organizational issues to emotional costs suffered by individuals who believe they cannot express or contribute their true intelligence and insight at work.

Tell me, I need to know

One highly respected manger we spoke to was known by his team as the "tell me, I need to know boss." What made him different? According to his team, he

- Persuasively encouraged active participation in the problem sharing/analysis process even if it took much time to do so
- Did not interrupt or cut across conversations
- Was vigilant in having all work through solution strategies
- Demanded full accountability for actions taken
- Required feedback from his team on how he performed

"We all speak up. The conversations are fierce. Nobody is put down. His confidence has infected us all," commented one of managers who clashed with his boss more than most.

Such examples remain in the minority. Silence is expensive, but many remain fearful for one reason or another of fierce conversations.

Ask Yourself

- Can and do people express themselves in your team?
- What do you do to actively generate confidence in voicing opinions?
- How do you know that you are not being told what you like to hear?

Take a diverse view of diversity

In the United States, diversity is predominantly a gender issue. But elsewhere in the world it can mean other things. In South Africa, diversity is all about race. How do you stand above political correctness?

Different strokes

Attitudes to diversity vary. In 2008, for example, 15 women ran Fortune 500 companies—an all-time high. In Greece most businesses are started by women. In China, too, women lead the field in entrepreneurship.

Among the 12,500 organizations in our top team research whether you were a man or a woman was the least predictive element of success. On the other hand, there is plenty of evidence to suggest that diversity of background among the top team enhances performance.

Global organizations are melting pots of emotion, argument, dispute, and disagreement. In order to not be swallowed up with strife and tension, any leader must acknowledge the diversity of views that exist within the top team. Then work toward reaching a meaningful conclusion on vision and strategy as a management team.

Indeed, being able to harness diversity is increasingly vital.[18] Look around. The Western world is reaching, and in many sectors has reached, a point of market maturity. In order to be more competitive, most organizations have invested in adopting the latest tools and techniques from sales, marketing to IT.

Yet, despite all that, for the consumer, differences of quality of service and product across a range of companies are minimal.

Effectively managing diversity in its widest sense can be an important differentiator. Inevitably, this is also likely to expose a greater disparity of views. The question is: is the clash of views generated by people with different backgrounds and points of view worth the effort required to reconcile those differences? Does your organization believe diversity creates real value or does it simply accept it is politically correct? Do you as a leader see it as an irritant or a competitive advantage?

These questions, we believe, lie at the heart of the diversity debate.[19] Sadly, they are rarely asked and even more rarely answered with any degree of honesty. Most organizations and leaders are mired in the organizational niceties of the gender issue rather than the commercial potential of a much broader interpretation and implementation of diversity.

Glass ceilings

Corporations may champion diversity, but the reality is that women are less likely to become a CEO than men. It would be nice to think that in the twenty-first century there was gender equality at the apex of the corporate hierarchy. The statistics tell a different story, however.

A 2007 report of Fortune Global 200 companies revealed women in just 11 percent of senior posts, and of companies with female board representation, nearly half had only one woman on the board. In Asia the situation is a particularly grim for women with CEO aspirations—5 out of 389 board seats at Fortune Global 200 companies in Japan were held by women. The more recent Heidrick and Struggles, *Boards in Turbulent Times*, Corporate Governance Report, 2009, identifies an interesting spread, with Sweden and Finland having 22 and 21 percent of women on boards respectively whilst Italy and Portugal have a measly 3 percent each. The European average is 10 percent.

Europe lags behind the United States in what little moves there are to appoint women directors. The list of the top companies with the highest percentage of women board directors, featured 18 U.S.-based companies, with 8 from Europe. The top two spots were taken by Netherlands-headquartered firm Royal Ahold, where women held four out of the seven seats on the supervisory board and Norway Statoil, where five out of ten board members were women.

Of the 45 companies without any female representation, 30 were Asian companies, including major brands such as Toyota, Nissan Motor, Hyundai, and Honda, as well as some major European corporations such as DaimlerChrysler and Fiat.

For those women who do make it to the top the news is not good, either. UK academics, Alexander Haslam and Michelle Ryan analyzed a correlation of the performance of FTSE 100 companies in the UK during 2003, with and without women on their boards. Their conclusion was that companies performing badly are more likely to appoint women to the board. Once performance recovers, companies are less likely to appoint women to the board. As a result women directors are often appointed at a difficult period and their appointment can easily be mistaken for a factor in the company's poor performance.

In other words, suggested Haslam and Ryan even when women do break through the unbreakable glass ceiling that they typically confront when climbing the corporate ladder, they often find themselves at the edge of a glass cliff.

In our travels we find that global leaders recognize that diversity isn't solely about gender. Nor is it just about race, or religion. And it certainly is not be about tolerance or tokenism. The whole point about diversity is that it manifests itself in diverse ways. In reality, it is about diversity of perspective more than anything else.

In Hong Kong a leading headhunter (a woman) explained to us: "The Western view of diversity is all about gender. When American companies say they want to talk about diversity it just irritates me. Gender is totally irrelevant to a Chinese woman living in Hong Kong. The correct question is: what does diversity mean in Shanghai or wherever? The meaning of diversity is linked to location and of course, business."

Celebrating diversity

There is an urgent need to recast diversity: from tolerance to celebration. The imperative to embrace diversity—cultural, religious, and political—has never been clearer or more urgent. Recent events have provided new impetus to actively promote and encourage diversity at the community, government, and business level. Many believe that what are needed are strategies to promote—and celebrate—diversity as a positive force in a globalized world.

In the business world there is a growing awareness that the ability to work in culturally diverse groups is increasingly key to success. Some commentators even refer to "diversity advantage." If the best software programmer lives in Bangalore you have to work with him or her no matter what. Doing business globally no longer means exporting your management model or view of the world, it requires sensitive management of people drawn from many background.

As already stated, in the past, debate about diversity tended to become mired in political correctness. In many cases the rights and wrongs of strategies such as positive discrimination have obscured the issues. Notwithstanding its tradition as a cultural melting pot, in the United States, in particular, attention has focused on racial divides, rather than the benefits of diversity. As a consequence diversity has been viewed as a problem rather than a solution.

This view, some commentators argue, is apparent in the way that American companies have sought to export their management model to other parts of the world. (Few commentators identify the ability to adjust to foreign cultures as a prime American advantage.) In Europe, on the other hand, diversity has tended to be a cultural rather than a racial issue. Getting along with other cultures is axiomatic to the modern European experience in the core countries of the European Union—France, Germany, Italy, Spain, Belgium, the Netherlands, the United Kingdom, Ireland, and Scandinavia. That doesn't mean that relations are always harmonious, but diversity is accepted as a fact of business life.

The diversity debate is now moving beyond calls for tolerance, to one that seeks to celebrate differences. There is a growing sense that a deep-seated respect for different perspectives and value systems is the key to an inclusive global society. The alternative is exclusion. Exclusion, many believe, results in alienation. Ultimately it can be corrosive, leading to extremism and even violence.

In the end, it is our differences that define us as human beings. The best hope for fostering shared understanding is the active engagement of diverse groups. Participation—in the work place, in the community, and in government—is best achieved through creating conditions that allow people to retain their identity and sense of self-worth. By celebrating diversity, we are better able to combine human talents and knowledge. Diversity offers a stronger gene pool. The reality of globalization, too, is that companies require an understanding of customers around the world. The case for diversity is compelling.

Nowhere more is this seen than in the corporate boards of Luxembourg, Switzerland, and the Netherlands, where more than 50 percent of directors are foreign nationals.[20]

Ask Yourself

- What does diversity mean for you?
- Is there a shared view of diversity within the organization?
- Who really believes in your diversity policies and practices?
- Does the diversity of your senior management reflect the diversity of your markets?
- What about your other stakeholders? Which stakeholders should you pay most attention to on diversity issues?
- Is diversity just PR in your organization or is it an integral part of your strategy?
- Do you assume it is a gender issue? Race issue?

Understand communication channels

Tune in to how people communicate in different places and situations.

Communicate or lose

What do corporate leaders actually do all day? Ask them and they will talk about strategies, visions, and missions. They will tell you about their endless traveling and their equally endless meetings, their packed diaries, how they haven't seen their children for days.

Press a little harder, and you will likely encounter a strained silence as they contemplate what they really do. The heart of leadership is not the esoteric world of strategizing but something more mundane and, as a result, largely ignored by educators, commentators, and, indeed, leaders. What leaders really do is communicate. Whether sending an email from a BlackBerry, giving a presentation to the board or to expectant analysts, scribbling a thank-you note to a high achiever, handling an annual appraisal, or just walking the corridors, a leader is always communicating.

But even though they spend most of their time communicating with people inside and outside the organization, leaders are rarely trained in the nuances of communication. Just look at the contents of an average MBA program, and you will see the usual heavyweight suspects: economics, strategy, marketing, accounting, and organizational behavior (often delivered as a highly esoteric lecture). Communication is the invisible elephant in the MBA classroom. In fact, an MBA graduate working in the corporate world will tell you that strategy is the easy bit; execution is the real challenge. What they will rarely add is that communication lies at the heart of executing anything, anywhere.

Take Kevin Kelly, CEO of the global search firm Heidrick & Struggles. Kelly is typical of the restlessly peripatetic, smart, modern CEO. "The reality is that every time I am on the move, I make a call. Every time I have a break, I call someone," he admits. "I go through a mental list of people I haven't spoken to for a while or someone I've worked with who has some news to share." His day features a stream of calls, one-on-ones, and group meetings with people inside and outside the organization. In short, his typical workday consists of communicating.

What must executives understand about communication to make it work for them? What marks out the best communicators from the executive crowd? Having worked with many leaders— from CEOs to B-school deans—over the past decade, former journalists and now visiting professors in communication at IE Business School in Madrid, Stuart Crainer and Des Dearlove have discovered that the most effective communicators master eight disciplines of leadership communication.

1   Always on

"The first point to recognize is that as the leader, you are communicating 24/7, and everything you do is amplified—and can be distorted. Everyone is watching you, taking a cue from you. Tiny things become important, so that the smallest gesture or the most flippant remark is examined minutely for a sign of your intentions. Even walking down the corridor is imbued with significance. Whom you stop to speak to—and whom you don't speak to—is regarded by others as noteworthy," say Dearlove and Crainer.

And then there are those outside the company: the media, financial analysts, shareholders. For the unwary CEO, an off-the-cuff remark over lunch can become a newspaper headline. Internally, too, an indiscreet whisper can reverberate.

A classic example of the dangers of nothing ever truly being off the record is that of the British executive Gerald Ratner. Ratner ran a highly successful nationwide chain of jewelers. It was a family company, something of a British institution. Successful and confident, Ratner made a 1991 speech at the Royal Albert Hall to a gathering of executives. He made a few jokes about the poor saps who had made him rich by buying his shoddy merchandise; some of the jewelry sold by his shops, he quipped, was "cheaper than an M&S prawn sandwich but probably wouldn't last as long." A tabloid newspaper journalist got hold of his speech, and the story made the front page. Ratner found himself on the back foot, and offended consumers quickly consigned his family retail chain to history.

Being the leader means having a permanently open microphone. Even your silences are audible. In uncertain times, silence is the most deafening of all messages. Communication, like nature, abhors a vacuum. Create one in your organization, and the rumor mill goes into overdrive to fill it. Noncommunication is not an option, so you must learn to live in a goldfish bowl. How you deal with it depends on your personality, but you must recognize that you are communicating even when you don't mean to. Smart leaders turn this to their advantage, making a virtue of what might otherwise be a vise.

Sir Martin Sorrell, CEO of WPP Group, the world's biggest advertising group, is famed for his rapid response to emails—whenever, wherever. "If someone contacts you, there's a reason," he insists. "It's got nothing to do with the hierarchy. It doesn't matter if they're not a big person. There's nothing more frustrating than a voice mail and then nothing back. We're in a service business." It's not unusual for Sorrell to spend a working week in the United States but remain on UK time for the benefit of his employees back in London. His attitude sends a clear message: If you work for me, then you are important.

2   Know your messages

Politicians talk about staying on message, and this is an equally valuable lesson for all leaders. Some will argue that spin doctoring is rife in political and corporate life, but it is not spin to be consistent in what you say. Consistency requires discipline. The best leaders we know put a great deal of effort into figuring out an organization's priorities and articulating them in a compelling way.

As well as coming up with the strategy, a leader has to communicate it to the organization. The best strategy in the world is useless unless it makes it out of the CEO's head and into the heads of the people who will make it happen. An appetite for repetition helps. The best leaders we have met are briefed to the hilt and can run through their key messages in their sleep. Being a leader is grunt work. You have to say the same thing time and time again to a variety of different audiences. You might emphasize a particular point for the media, for employees or analysts, but the message must remain consistent.

3   Think audience

Put yourself in the position of your audience. For example, financial analysts aren't interested in grand visions of a better world—they want to know the numbers. Conversely, employees want to be inspired. There is a classic YouTube video clip that features an overexcited and sweating Steve Ballmer taking the stage at a Microsoft event and proclaiming that he loves the company. To outsiders, Ballmer's hyperkinetic delivery is risible; for Microsoft employees it has a more positive effect: Here is someone who has energy and total belief in the company.

Above all, people crave meaning. Google employees—most of them, anyway—are motivated not by how much money the company is making but by the notion that they are making a difference. For them, the (neatly distilled) corporate slogan "do no evil" is more important than next quarter's results.

4   Distill it

It is not enough to simply know your messages. You have to be able to communicate them concisely. Effective communicators are masters of distillation. Like a fine bourbon, they take their key messages and boil them down to their essence. Messages that are pithy and memorable are easiest to communicate.

At GE, Jack Welch never got enough credit for his mastery of communication. One of his most underrated skills was his ability to distill a clear message and repeat it endlessly. His time at GE can be divided into three eras, with three simple messages. The first era was characterized by his message that each of GE's businesses must be No. 1 or No. 2 in market share in its industry. During the second era—along with a focus on Six Sigma and Work-Out—he insisted that those same businesses define their markets so that their share was no greater than 10 percent, thereby forcing managers to look for new opportunities beyond the confines of a narrowly conceived market. In the final era, with the internet changing the business world, he summed up his message in the phrase, "Destroy your own business before someone else does."

5 Find your own voice

Great communicators are authentic communicators. Few people are brilliant across all communications channels. Not everyone can command the rapt attention of a one-thousand-seat auditorium. Effective leaders know their strengths—and their weaknesses. Some prefer the 20-seat seminar room; others like communication to be one-on-one. What's important is that the leader chooses an effective medium to transmit desired messages.

Think of Franklin D. Roosevelt. When he needed to communicate his New Deal to ordinary Americans in a way that inspired hope and confidence, he invented a new form of radio broadcast. His fireside chats were ideally suited to his communication strengths: informal and personable. Great leaders find their most effective media.

And consider Virgin's Richard Branson. Despite years on public stages, Branson's delivery tends to be faltering; public speaking is not his forte. And yet he is instantly recognized throughout the world and is a highly effective communicator of his company's key values. What Branson figured out years ago was that his willingness to make a fool of himself and to try things other CEOs wouldn't contemplate is actually a powerful statement of Virgin's brand values—different, colorful, iconoclastic, and fun-loving. Branson dressing as a Virgin bride, hamming it up as a spaceman, or abseiling down skyscrapers is great communication.

Visiting an executive's office in Tokyo, we were struck by a handwritten letter on the wall, proudly framed and displayed—a thank-you note from Jack Welch, our host proudly explained. Welch famously wrote handwritten notes to congratulate and thank people he came across. Another CEO we met spent all his time when in the back of his limo scribbling notes to be faxed to people when he arrived at his destination. Of course, communication is now easy. You can send mass emails at the touch of a key to everyone in an organization. Sometimes these are appropriate. As with everything, context is all.

6 Tell stories

People have used storytelling to communicate important messages for as long as they have been able to speak. Human beings are hardwired for narrative; it provides meaning. Facts and figures provide content but can never replace context.

From the earliest times, people have used stories to communicate important messages. Whether told by tribal elders around the campfire or by wandering minstrels, stories were used to pass on collective memories before people could read or write. Often they had a purpose beyond simple entertainment; even fairy tales, for example, usually contain a grain of wisdom or warning. Today, the power of stories is increasingly recognized in business. General Electric, Royal Dutch/Shell, IBM, Unilever, and Nestlé are among the companies that explicitly use storytelling in their communications.

Every leader needs a narrative that addresses: Who am I? What do I stand for? Where we are going? And what does all this mean to followers? Effective communicators recognize that communication must appeal to the head and the heart. The head is about making a rational case, using hard facts, but it is the heart that commits to action. As Terry Pearce, a highly respected executive coach and leadership-communications expert, says: "While the mind looks for proof, the heart looks for engagement. While the mind looks for information, the heart looks for passion. While the mind looks for answers, the heart looks for experience. The mind makes a decision, and it's the heart that makes a commitment."

7   Use symbols

What we say as leaders is important. But people also judge their leaders by what they do. Actions speak loudest. Take the 1995 Rugby World Cup final between South Africa and New Zealand. The tournament was held in South Africa and was seen as an affirmation of the nation's move from being an international pariah to a modern democratic nation. Rugby was traditionally a game played by the white Afrikaans population. The black population played and followed soccer.

The final was attended by newly elected president Nelson Mandela, wearing a green and gold South African rugby uniform. His message was simple: White or black, we are all South Africans now. Mandela's team beat the hot favorites, a victory for unity.

Effective communicators recognize the power of symbolic actions. When the pharmaceutical company Roche was beset by takeover rumors, instead of fielding the long line of media requests for an interview, CEO Franz Humer stuck to his weekend plan to go skiing. His message was that he was unconcerned by the takeover talk and in control of the situation. This was dutifully reported by the media, and the rumor mill speedily ground to a halt.

Symbolic communication can also be more mundane. Where leaders park their cars speaks volumes about the organization's culture. If the CEO parks his Mercedes right next to the front door while everyone else has to traipse across a vast parking lot, they might conclude that hierarchy is alive and well—despite the CEO's lip service to a flat management structure. When Greg Dyke became director-general of the BBC in 2000, he inherited a demoralized organization with a top-heavy management structure. One of his first actions was to get rid of the chauffeur-driven cars allocated to senior executives. It sent a clear message that cost-cutting started at the top rather than the bottom.

8 Stay in touch

Perhaps the hardest discipline of all for leaders is staying in touch with stakeholders, both internal and external. It is relatively easy for leaders in the early days because they remember what it was like to not be a leader. Over time, of course, that memory fades. The best leaders work hard at staying in touch. The most underestimated communication discipline: listening. For some leaders, listening is simply the noise before they speak. But people are able to spot a leader who is just going through the motions.

Great leaders are great listeners. They hear what people have to say and use that information to inform their decisions and their communication. Nor do they become captivated by their advisors or by those who speak the loudest. Upon stepping down, UK Prime Minister Tony Blair noted: "The hardest thing about leadership is learning to ignore the loudest voices." The greatest irony of great communication is that when you don't think you are communicating, you may be communicating your most powerful message of all.

Only connecting

To these points, we would add the following observations.

First, communication should always be personal and the more personal you can make it the more effective it is likely to be. "If you talk to a man in a language he understands, that goes to his head. If you talk to him in his language, that goes to his heart," says Nelson Mandela.[21]

Second, in the business world every act of communication has a business objective. That objective may be about building relationships and network but it is still, nevertheless, a business objective.

Third, communication is contextual. Different contexts require very different channels of communication. Cross-cultural understanding is about more than just understanding the language that is spoken; it is also about the way we communicate and the channels we use to communicate. "In order for business leaders to lead effectively in intercultural situations, they must engage and interact with those cultures in whose countries they work with a desire to understand and appreciate that culture and its people," observes E. S. Wibbeke in his book, *Global Business Leadership*.[22]

Fourth, but certainly not last, communication is how you get anything done. Without communication, nothing happens, the greatest strategy on earth remains a neat theory. "We had the board minutes; it's all written and then printed out for the next board meeting. But that is not what makes us effective. Our board decisions, whether as a result of expression of views or protracted discussion, are determined by information and analysis which is the heart of our governance. Documents and agendas are a pretext which can be changed. Discussion, well sourced information and agreement are what make us successful," one Turkish board member told us.

The context's the thing

In communication, one size does not fit all. For example, Western businesses entering the Indian market struggle to grasp the concept that India has a tradition of verbal communication in business.

The importance of India's long oral tradition is evident from the world-renowned epic poem the Mahabharata, which was, according to legend, related by Vyasa, and recorded on palm leaf manuscripts by the elephant-headed Ganesha using his tusk as a pen. The Indian people most commonly experience the

Mahabharata in the form of a narration. And the ancient Indian texts called the Vedas, fundamental to the Hindu religion, are "sruti"—or that which is heard.

The Indian love of the spoken word became clear to one French student on an internship with an Indian software company, when the student noticed that while he was busy diligently taking notes in all his meetings, his colleagues didn't write down meeting minutes, or project plans, and yet everyone still seemed to know what to do and when.

While there were telephone conversations a plenty, there was very little note taking. Despite the lack of written planning, the software project was completed on schedule. The client, though, didn't bother to check the requirement document against the finished product, but just wanted to know that it worked. In the weeks that followed, the client relied less on manuals and screenshots and more on constant phone calls, resolving any problems through verbal discussion.

Verbal communication is key to success in the Indian business environment. This reliance on the spoken word might be attributable to poor levels of literacy, or alternatively a dislike of the permanence of the written word in a country where truth can be, in many cases, a shifting concept depending on context. But, it means that email messages are not enough when it comes to team leadership. Instead verbal communication is mandatory, face-to-face if it is an important issue.

So whereas idle gossip, chit-chat, storytelling, and other forms of verbal communication around the office might be frowned upon in some cultures, in India at least it appears that they are part of creating an effective workplace. In a world where work communication seems to be increasingly dominated by the written world whether it is email or text messaging, that's a refreshing thought.

The noted anthropologist and cross-cultural researcher, Edward Twitchell Hall Jr, differentiated between low- and high-context communication. High-context and low-context communication refers to how much speakers rely on things other than words to convey meaning. Hall states that in communication, individuals face many more sensory cues than they are able to fully process. In each culture, members have been supplied with specific "filters" that allow them to focus only on what society has deemed important.

In general, cultures that favor low-context communication will pay more attention to the literal meanings of words than to the context surrounding them. Low-context communication focuses on verbal elements and is characteristic of cultural groups from North America, the United Kingdom, and Germany.

High-context communication, blends low verbal messages with a lot of bodily behavior, motions, and signs. This typifies Central and Eastern Europe, the Mediterranean region, South America, among others.

Nonverbal behavior elements include the following:

- Eye contact
- Facial expression
- Posture and gestures
- Distance between interlocutors
- Influence of odors
- Tempo and time factors
- Touch
- Artifacts and environmental objects

Highs and lows

As individuals, all of us use both high-context and low-context communication. Often, the types of relationships we have with others and the situation will determine the extent to which we rely more on literal or implied meanings.

To better understand high-context and low-context communication, ask the following:

Do I recognize implied messages from others, and am I aware of the verbal *and* nonverbal cues that let me understand the speaker's meaning? (High-Context)

Do I "let my words speak for themselves?" Do I prefer to be more direct, relying on what is explicitly stated in my speech? (Low-Context)

Novelist Amy Tan describes the differences in cultural communication this way: "An American business executive may say, 'Let's make a deal,' and the Chinese manager may reply, 'Is your son interested in learning about your widget business?' Each to his or her own purpose, each with his or her own linguistic path."

When individuals from high-context and low-context cultures collaborate, the potential for misunderstandings is large. These problems can be separated into differences concerning "direction," "quantity," and "quality." For example, employees from high-context cultures like China and France share very specific and extensive information with their "in-group members"— friends, family, and close colleagues. In comparison, low-context cultures like the United States and Germany prefer to limit communication to smaller, more select groups of people, sharing only that information which is necessary.

Words and pictures

Even an apparently straightforward task, such as translating a message from one language into another, can be full of cultural pitfalls, as research by Nader Tavassoli, professor of marketing, at London Business School highlights.

With a market of over a billion potential consumers, it is no surprise that the issue of how to advertise effectively in China is high on the agenda of Western-based multinational corporations, and their advertising agencies.

Reaching those consumers is no easy matter, however. The cross-cultural challenges of branding and marketing relate to the most apparently simple of issues—the translation of branding copy in English into its Chinese logograph counterpart.

With over 10,000 logographs each corresponding to a single spoken syllable, the Chinese language is visually rich in a way that English is not. A different approach is required in China to get over the brand message from that which might be used in the United States or the United Kingdom.

To ensure maximum impact through the use of branding and advertising messages in Chinese, marketers need to be aware of a number of issues.

So, for example, reading logographs involves more visual processing than reading text. As a result, visual features such as colors assume greater significance in branding. The downside for Western retailers is that the strong connection between color and brand means that creating copycat brands is easier when you are using Chinese logographs.

Chinese consumers are also more sensitive to the fonts used than their Western counterparts. They are, for example, more attuned to the perceived femininity or masculinity of fonts. It is far easier to slip-up by using a masculine font to advertise a new lipstick, with consequent disappointing sales performance.

The spatial location of design elements also assumes greater significance to a Chinese consumer. And so changes in design layout may trigger unexpected responses.

Western advertisements frequently use music, jingles, and other audio elements in conjunction with linguistic elements to create a brand image. In China, however, visual elements such as logos and other design elements are so important that these, rather than sounds, are likely to have a greater impact in terms of ad retrieval cues.

Indeed it is not just China that places an emphasis on color. In their paper "The Colours of Anger, Envy, Fear, and Jealousy: A Cross-Cultural Study," Ralph Hupka and fellow academics explored the different cultural associations between words representing emotion and colors.

Over 600 people in Germany, Mexico, Poland, Russia, and the United States were asked to indicate on a six-point scale to what extent anger, envy, fear, and jealousy reminded them of 12 different colors.

While there was a degree of agreement between the different nationals—the colors of anger were black and red, fear was black, and jealousy was red—there was also significant disagreement. Envy, for example, was associated with purple by the Poles; black, purple, and yellow by the Russians; black, green, and red by the Americans; and yellow by the Germans. In China be careful when bringing gifts to the home. Yellow is for baby girls and pink for baby boys.

The researchers concluded that such difference in word association were driven by culture-specific variables such as language, mythology, and literature.

The medium *is* the message

Marshall McLuhan may have had a point when he linked the medium and the message in his book *Understanding Media: The Extensions of Man*, but the world was a lot less complicated in 1964. What would McLuhan have made of the global village (another term he coined) in 2010? Long gone are the days when the choice of medium was comparatively restricted, whether it was radio, television, books, magazines, landlines or that archaic form of communication—the letter.

Today, the business landscape is cluttered with communication options available to executives. Technological advances mean more communication options are on hand for the average executive than ever. Instant messaging, email, fax, landline, mobile, voice over internet, video conferencing, twittering, the list goes on. Whether sending or receiving, executives the world over face a bewildering array of communication and collaboration tools to use every day at work, and at home. And the more methods of communication there are, the more scope for cultural confusion.

Luckily, for the world's workers help may be at hand. The next big thing in ICT is unified communications—technology that allows video, instant messaging, email, video and other communications tools to be accessed not through zillions of individual application, but instead through a single interface.

Besides narrowing down the number of ways to present a message clumsily, inappropriately, or incorrectly, to a colleague or customer elsewhere in the world, unified communications technology cuts communication costs by 10 percent, increases productivity by 10 percent, and improves customer satisfaction by 21 percent.[23] Six out of ten people said that unified communications was a major factor in promoting collaboration, making the business more efficient, and working more flexible. Those are the kinds of figures that make sense in any country.

Perhaps one day we will all be using technology like Cisco's TelePresence system. TelePresence is the Formula 1 of video conferencing. Straight out of a sci-fi novel it beams a life-size image of the person you are communicating right into the room with you. It enables you to have a conversation with a high resolution, Dolby stereo, virtual expert advisor, just as if they were sitting across the conference table from you.

Consign verbal misunderstandings over the phone, or errant emails, to the waste-bin. In Cisco's vision of the future the quality of the virtual image of the person you are dealing with is so good you can make direct eye contact with it, and engage in all the other body language that accompanies human interaction, even though the participants in the dialog may be tens of thousands of miles away from each other. You may be on assignment on the other side of the world, but in the real-time collaborative communication future, there is no hiding from the boss.

Whatever the technology, at the heart of communication is emotional intelligence, the sensitivity to tune into the communication methods, habits, and limitations of others.

Our research strongly highlights the importance of interactive and communicative skills. They cannot be ignored.

Ask Yourself

- How do you communicate?
- Which communication channel do you use most and which do you use most effectively?
- Which communication channel are you uncomfortable with?
- How adept are you at changing communication channels?

Privacy and confidentiality

Privacy and confidentiality have very different meanings around the globe. What can and can't you say?

Fairly private

What does the word privacy or secret mean? Or confidentiality? Actually, we have no idea. Confidentiality in the stakeholder culture means it is confidential to that network. But where does that network extend to? Confidentiality in an individualistic culture means a completely different thing.

Privacy exists in many contexts—personal, financial, and informational. Fundamentally it is about noninterference; the freedom to do what one wants, free of unilateral intervention and judgment by third-parties. It is closely linked to ideas about the sanctity of private property.

Privacy is a concept which has traditionally been strong in societies where the role of the individual is strong, as opposed to the collective. Protection of private property is also high. It has appeared to be an Anglo-Saxon obsession, perhaps strongest in Protestant cultures where more emphasis is placed on the individual aspects of religious belief.

The importance of understanding the different interpretations of privacy and confidentiality has been brought home to us time and time again. We were in Shanghai and went to one of the oldest tea houses. It was a beautiful place by a lake. It was very formal. All the tables were carefully set out. Someone on another table started talking to us. Our Chinese guide said, "Why don't we turn all the tables around, and bring them all together, so we can all talk?" For the Chinese, to take the whole room and completely change it so that we all share was completely natural. And for them, our reaction—slightly perplexed about why we were talking to these complete strangers—was unnatural.

In Southall, West London, the population is 90 percent Indian or Bangladeshi extraction. There are lots of old Sikhs walking around. On the benches at the side of the road, typically you would just have one bench. But in Southall, there are two benches looking at each other. You never get that anywhere else in the United Kingdom, but that is the natural way of things for the people who live there.

The private English

Let's take a world tour and begin with our adopted homeland and the ever so private English.

In England the law (whether Common Law or Statute) gave the individual numerous rights and procedures for defending them. In particular the tort of trespass (and the more restricted tort of nuisance) developed. An Englishman's home is his castle after all.

The home was central to this world. The Englishman or woman owned this place, whether it was an extensive estate or a humble semi-detached dwelling in soulless suburbia. It was where privacy mattered most. It was where those dearest were also nearest; where they could be protected from harm or interference.

The desire to own a home is still one of the greatest motivations in the United Kingdom, as shown by the jump in owner-occupier dwellings between 1971 and 2006. At the earlier date, owner-occupation was already high at 51 percent, yet by 2006 it had risen to 70 percent. Home ownership is worth working for, to the extent that people are prepared to make sacrifices to service often crippling mortgage payments.

Another facet of privacy is ownership of the private motor car. This gives people a small, often inconvenient mobile space. You

don't have to share it with anyone, apart maybe from your partner or kids, but then that's never a violation of privacy. These
are people who are essential parts of the private space.

Technological improvements, especially in the ability to handle
large databases, have created the demand for informational privacy. In the United Kingdom this led to the Data Protection Act
1998. This concerns itself with personal data and so acknowl-
edges that such information is something over which the individual has a proprietary right before any other body. Not only
do you own your own home and car, your data belongs to you
first of all. Interestingly though, privacy is never mentioned
once in the act.

The reality in the United Kingdom of the twenty-first century
is that all telephone, text, and email messages are logged and
kept for 12 months and are made available to no fewer than 652
public bodies for their use and investigation.[24] This intrusion is
now affecting all citizens, communities, and businesses across
the world. With privacy so built into their way of thinking, why
aren't the British reacting more to such intrusion?

The not-so-private Americans

And now, the not-so-private Americans. It goes without saying
that the United States should be a place where the protection of
personal privacy should be pursued with vigor.

As early as 1789 future president James Madison introduced an
amendment to the constitution—the fourth—which guaranteed
"the right of the people to be secure in their persons, houses,
papers and effects, against unreasonable searches and seizures."
The individualist aspect of privacy, and the right to the unfet-
tered enjoyment of private property, has been a fundamental
U.S. value. It was seen to be under threat from technology, first
the printing press and then from a host of technological devices
which promised at one level to make life better but which could,
in the wrong hands, become the levers of tyranny. In 1890 two
eminent jurists, Samuel Warren and Louis Brandeis, published

a seminal article in the *Harvard Law Review* entitled "The Right to Privacy." They wrote:

> *That the individual shall have full protection in person and in property is a principle as old as the Common Law; but it has been found necessary from time to time to define anew the exact nature and extent of such protection.*

Warren and Brandeis were particularly worried about the proliferation of new reproductive media, like printing presses and cameras. The advent of technologies like the internet has raised fresh concerns. Technology is seen as the means by which personal privacy can be undermined. In the Kyllo judgment of June 2001 the U.S. Supreme Court found that the use of thermal imaging equipment without a warrant, ostensibly to detect marijuana cultivation in private dwellings, constituted a violation of privacy. The deployment of the equipment was construed by the court to be a search, which, according to the fourth amendment, could not be carried out without a warrant.

Europe's open door policy

But privacy is not just an Anglo-Saxon fixation. In Europe the European Convention on Human Rights' Article 8 specifically guarantees respect for private and family life, as well as asserting the inviolability of the home and of private correspondence. Although the European Court of Human Rights has done a lot to expand the remit of Article 8, the convention as a whole can be seen as a document which reacted to the totalitarianism of the 1930s and 1940s, and which aimed through the prescription of certain activities to preclude another European war.

The European Union's interest in privacy has understandably been confined to informational aspects and data protection. The means adopted has been an EU directive 95/46/EC which cannot have any effect until transposed into the municipal legislation of member states.

Attitudes to privacy differ across continental Europe. In France issues surrounding informational privacy and identity theft were already burning issues in the 1970s. In 1978 a special government agency *La Commission national de l'informatique et des libertés* was set up to monitor compliance with data protection laws. Even with this body there has always been an unspoken assumption that notions of individual privacy should and would be overridden in the interests of government policy.

French people have an ambiguous attitude toward privacy. On the one hand they do not seem to worry so much about it as *les rosbifs*, but when it is endangered there can be an outcry, as occurred when a radio station tried to air a program called *SOS Delation*. This basically encouraged members of the public to inform on their friends and neighbors, and be indiscrete about extra-marital affairs or undeclared income. The reaction was so vociferous and hostile that the program was quietly shelved.

It can be heightened by religious considerations. Anyone who has ever taken a walk around a Dutch town at night is often struck by the absence of window curtains on many houses. The traditional reason for this—allegedly—is that in the old days curtains were frowned upon by church ministers. The faithful—and anyone else leading a sinless life that they weren't ashamed of—didn't need to hide what was going on behind pieces of fabric. This would have been a denial of privacy in English eyes.

Screaming Spaniards

Spanish society has always placed a lot of emphasis on the collective, so privacy was not important there or in Latin America. This is still the case, there are parts of Barcelona which have the highest concentration of human beings in Europe with single multistoreyed tower blocs being home to maybe a thousand and more people. These are fairly well built, but they are never soundproof. A scene in an Almodovar film pretends to show the National Screaming Contests, a back-handed tribute to the allegation that the Spaniards are amongst the noisiest people on earth!

What happens in Spain is not the negation of a need for privacy. It is placed in context. It is something which can be enjoyed and savored. It doesn't need structures. It is enjoyable in the middle of a crowded square just as much as by yourself.

Niet **to privacy**

It is a good indication of the different attitudes to privacy in Russia that there is no word for privacy in the Russian language. The closest is *neprikosnovennost' chastnoy zhiz'ni* or noninvolvement with confidential life—a bit of a mouthful. Russian society has never given the individual much power. Collective organizations—the state, the party, the Orthodox church, and going further back the village—have always been more important.

And then, during the Soviet period, privacy was viewed as akin to private property. It was a petit-bourgeois anachronism like private emotions. It was limiting and ultimately counter-revolutionary. Resignation to the will of the collective, to the extent that this might even lead to the extinction of private identity, had to be embraced. The means of production were collectivized, as were the strands of everyday life.

During the Stalin years a family was lucky indeed if it could get a one-room flat to live in. More common was having to share spaces, demarcated by washing-lines or flimsy curtains. And even those with spaces of their own often had to share communal kitchens. These *kolechnie* were the scenes of innumerable squabbles over allegations of pilfering of precious food items.

Even when more housing units were built, beginning with Khrushchev, these were often cramped spaces in draughty high-rise poorly built apartment blocks with permanently out-of-order lifts. The communal kitchens may have disappeared but the walls were often paper-thin.

Little if anything has changed since the fall of communism. Indeed there is much nostalgia for the "good old days," with their discomforts. At least you had a roof (albeit diaphanously thin and leaking) over your head.

Some people even miss the KGB. During the communist era, it was said that every sixth person in Russia was KGB. This wasn't as bad as it sounds. Most of the individuals in teams knew exactly who their KGB operative was. In fact, the KGB operative often acted more as a worker representative than a workplace spy. Think more along the lines of a trade union representative or shop steward. So the KGB member was known and was often quite popular. He or she was the person that you went to talk to, about political issues but also about personal, family, and social issues. So if their children weren't performing well at school, many people went to their KGB operative to discuss the issues. So, in Russia, the system of spying on people was integrated with the social development of communities and teams. Many individuals actually found that quite attractive and had problems readjusting once the communist system broke down and a capitalist system took over.

Today, however, the cult of the individual, and with it the desire for privacy, is gaining ground. Private car ownership has mushroomed in Russia. In 1990 the number of cars per one thousand people was 60; by 2004 it had risen to 160 per thousand people. It can seem that most of these are on the road when the traveler tries to get from the center of Moscow to their flight at Sheremetyevo airport. For those who now have a car they are the kings (maybe Tsars) of the road. The car may be a death-trap, held together with Scotch tape, and the drivers' behavior is often a demonstration of the most extreme and childish individualism.

Aspects of privacy will continue to be pursued avidly by those who can afford them. Their acquisition will be seen as progressive, leaving the past—with its discomforts and restrictions— firmly behind. For many the break from the past is symbolized by being able to travel to work in their own car, playing their stereo as loudly as they choose, instead of having to stand on an overcrowded and rickety Hungarian-made trolleybus.

For many, these aspirations will remain just that—dreams. But even in the most collective and previously anti-individualist society, the brave individual was always admired. Strong individuals showing physical and moral courage were seen as heroes. Such people passed into legend and tales of their derring-do were told wherever people met. It was an antidote to the prevailing collectivism—and still is. People admire what they know is unusual and what they know they can never really become.

In Stalin's time, the heroic individual was lionized in the figure of Aleksei Stakhanovite. On August 31, 1935, Stakhanovite, a 30-year-old miner working at the Central Irmino Mine in the Donets Basin, hewed 102 tons of coal during his 6-hour shift. This amount represented 14 times his quota, and within a few days of the feat it was hailed by *Pravda* as a world record.

It was further enhanced in the cult of the War Hero, like sniper Fyodor Okhlopkov. Their acts of individual sacrifice could be reconciled with the pursuit of collective goals—the Five-Year Plan or the War against Fascism. Yet respect for such individuals has continued, even though their aims are much more selfish.

In contemporary Russia, many oligarchs have taken on this role. Roman Abramovich's rise from humble beginnings to being one of the world's richest men is told and retold. Mikhail Khodorkovsky enjoys the same sort of cachet, probably enhanced since his very public fall from grace and subsequent imprisonment.

Confucian confusion

China has the world's highest population. For very practical reasons, societies with high volumes of people traditionally set little store on privacy. The influence of Confucian thinking has also been strong. This includes respect for authority, seniority, and family. The family and the state have always been of higher value than the individual and allied notions of privacy. Personal names always begin with the family name. This is used by all but the most intimate family members, maybe preceded by some honorific title. The individual could seldom rely with confidence on his own abilities, and had to look to family for support. This was heightened by China's history of economic and political crises, accompanied by incessant warfare and grinding famine. In the period between 1949 and 1978 the People's Republic of China placed huge emphasis on the collective and the individual's rights were often obliterated. Your status was dependant on the group to which you were assigned by the party. This might be an agricultural brigade or a work collective in a factory.

Since China began its rapprochement with the West and the adoption of capitalism, Western notions of privacy have increased in stature. Some of this was a deliberate reaction against the past, or a response to greater individual prosperity. Private ownership, for long outlawed, is now a fact of life in China, whether it is of places to live or means of transport. Yet, some Chinese dislike what is happening as they link wealth with crime and corruption. Under Mao they were given the chance to progress which they could never have had under a capitalist regime.

What is more "creature comforts" like stereo equipment and mobile phones are now avidly sought by younger Chinese. Chinese sociologist Lu Yao-Huai has said that the adoption of Western-style concepts of privacy will continue.[25] However, the result will continue to be something that has Chinese characteristics. Privacy will be pursued as an "instrumental good," useful in itself, but to be contrasted with something which is intrinsically good.

Big brother is here

Our world tour of privacy reveals some of the issues which peripatetic business people encounter every day. Behind this there is an even bigger issue: the impact of technology on privacy. In 1984 there were muted celebrations to mark the year in which George Orwell's nightmarish novel of the future was set.[26] The Orwellian world of Big Brother looking ominously over the shoulder of every citizen appeared a distant specter. Computers were in their infancy, satellites still held a certain novelty, and the only cameras you saw were on holiday.

Nearly a quarter of a century later and Orwell's vision appears chillingly real. Accelerated by 9/11, popularized by reality TV, we are in the midst of a global surveillance society. Look around.

Start with your computer. HTTP cookies communicate between websites and your computer. They save your preferences and help you shop online. Of course, there may be other uses for such information. Sitting comfortably at home you can enjoy the benefits of technology such as TiVo and Skyplus which know all about your viewing habits. At work, calls are routinely recorded. If you work in a call center, your boss could well be listening in to ensure you stick to the sales script rather than indulging in time-wasting conversation.

And there is much, much more. Credit card transactions, store loyalty cards, and mobile phones can all help pinpoint where we are and what we're doing. CCTV cameras have spread like measles throughout the developed world. The United Kingdom has 4.2 million CCTV cameras. If you do the maths, this works out at 1 camera for every 14 people. There are even tracking devises in shopping tags. Radio frequency tags mean that retail chains can monitor stock levels. They can also be used for other purposes. The UK retail chain Tesco has used an RFID tracking system to trigger CCTV coverage. The moment a customer picked up a pack of Gillette Mach 3 razor blades the tag activated a camera. The Department of Homeland Security in the United States and dozens of medical facilities now encourage the use of various types of RFID microchips all of which can be implanted under the skin. All our investigations confirm our worst fears. RFID tagging of humans is on the increase. Some have given permission. Others are oblivious to the fact. RFID and other tagging technologies are undoubtedly going to pose a major ethical challenge for business and government leaders.[27]

There is a certain irony in the fact that the surveillance society we live in is now itself being monitored, a case of Big Brother's Little Brother. Kirstie Ball of Open University Business School is one of those leading academic research into the surveillance explosion. She is part of an academic team called the Surveillance Project. The project, based at Queens University,

Kingston, Canada, is a multidisciplinary and international attempt to find out what happens to our personal data and how personal data processing impacts on our lives. The four-year multimillion dollar project maps attitudes to privacy across nine countries. "Surveillance is not simply about large organizations using sophisticated computer equipment," the project's website explains. "It is also about how ordinary people—citizens, workers, travellers and consumers—interact with surveillance. Some comply, others negotiate, and yet others resist."

The Globalization of Personal Data project is the first multicountry study of attitudes to privacy. One person's notion of privacy is different from his neighbor's, but there are cultural generalizations. Says Kirstie Ball: "There are two polar extremes of how we view privacy. At one extreme, privacy is seen as an unalienable right unaltered by us being at our place of work. At the other extreme it is seen as acceptable that when people go to work they surrender their rights to privacy. The US is keen on the latter approach—hence the use of drugs tests at work—while China is the country which is most in the rights direction."

Surveillance (defined as "any systematic collection of personal data on a person's life aimed at exerting influence over it") is nothing new. "Essential to bureaucracy is the oversight of subordinates and the creation of records. Business practices of double-entry book-keeping and of trying to cut costs and increase profit accelerated and reinforced such surveillance," says *A Report on the Surveillance Society* written by Kirstie Ball, David Lyon, David Wood, Clive Norris, and Charles Raab. Over a century ago, Henry Ford had a Sociology of Work Department which looked at the behavior in and out of work of Ford employees.

Things have moved on. Cars now come in different colors, and surveillance is omnipresent. There are undoubtedly unhealthy extremes. Experts now talk of "dataveillance," an Orwellian phrase if there ever was one. The good news is that the debate is underway. The surveillance society may lead to transparent tomorrows, we hope.

Ask Yourself

- Do you appreciate what privacy and confidentiality mean in different contexts? (Even how close you can stand to someone without invading their personal space?)
- When you tell someone that something is confidential, do you really understand what you are communicating in that culture?
- When you bring someone into your confidence, do you realize that by excluding others you may be insulting them?
- Do you realize that in some places—China, for example—being inside a confidence circle is important to an individual's status?
- What is the difference between commercial and personal confidentiality?
- When are privacy and confidentiality issues in conflict?

Respond to age-old issues

Age is viewed very differently around the world. In the West, older managers are regarded as past it and best pushed aside—though this is changing. In the East, age is revered and older managers are seen as the repositories of wisdom and brokers of power networks—and this, too, is changing.

Dancing pigs

In the autumn and early winter of 2008 television viewers in the United Kingdom avidly followed the performance of veteran political commentator John Sergeant (aged 64) in the BBC TV reality show *Strictly Come Dancing*. While his skills as a dancer left a lot to be desired, and led to him being unkindly branded as a dancing pig, audiences were enthralled by his commitment, especially when compared with the dancing of his fellow competitors, often lithe athletic models and sports stars some thirty or forty years his junior.

The Great British public also seemed to delight in contradicting the often harsh and unfair criticisms of the panel of experts who every week delivered comments of increasingly intolerant invective against Sergeant. When one of the judges Len Goodman (also aged 64), said that he made his comments because he wasn't working for "Help the Aged" he was roundly booed. Sergeant eventually withdrew from the contest, citing the unusual fear that he might win it—"a joke too far" as he described it.

The United Kingdom displays many of the contradictory impulses that affect how age is viewed. Despite encouraging the dancing skills of the mature political journalist, a similar tolerance is not extended to British political leaders. Indeed, there is an increasing intolerance of age among politicians. One of the reasons that led Sir Menzies Campbell (67) to resign as leader of the Liberal Democratic Party was continuous criticism of his age. Yet, Winston Churchill was 82 when he retired. Also in her eighties is Queen Elizabeth II, whose mother still fulfilled her official engagements well past her hundredth year. The message seems to be that old people will get respect, so long as they don't do anything important in national life (except for female royalty and war heroes). For senior citizens, dancing on television and waving from open topped cars are both acceptable: running the country or a major company is not.

Older and out?

To be fair, there are some valid reasons why age is not always synonymous with wisdom. One is that age can blunt curiosity and lead to what is described as "fighting the last war."

Says Phil Hodgson, director of leadership programs at the business school Ashridge: "Older leaders need to work very hard not to let their decision making and their understanding of a situation be dominated by their past experience of success and failure. It is very hard to accept that what worked before may not, probably will not, work as well again. Equally, what failed last time, does not necessarily define what will fail this time. The successful older leader stays successful by reinventing themselves so that they employ the learning without deploying the methods gleaned from yesteryear."

The issue of age also occupies the mind of Warren Bennis. Now in his late seventies, Bennis has grey hairs in abundance. As well as thinking about leadership, Bennis is a leader. During the Second World War, he was the youngest infantry officer in the U.S. Army in Europe. "It shaped me so much and pulled from me things I may never have experienced," Bennis recalls. "I was very shy and felt that I was a boring human being and then, in the course of being in the army, I felt that I was more interesting to myself. It was a coming of age—though I still didn't feel as though I was a leader."

For Bennis the war was what he calls a "crucible"—"utterly transforming events or tests that individuals must pass through and make meaning from in order to learn, grow, and lead." The trouble for youthful leaders is that crucibles are rare and cannot be artificially reproduced. You can't re-create Nelson Mandela's Robben Island.

Bennis' book, *Geeks and Geezers* (co-authored with Robert Thomas) examines a selection of "geeks," leaders between the ages of 21 and 35, and "geezers," men and women between the ages of 70 and 93. For many of the older leaders, the war and the depression were crucibles in which their values were formed.

"The geezers were brought up in survival mode," Bennis explains. "Often they grew up in some poverty with limited financial aspirations. They thought that earning $10,000 a year would have been enough. Compare that to the geeks some of whom made a lot of money when they were young. They are operating out of a different context. If the geeks were broke they would be more concerned with making a living than making history."

The message for would-be leaders is that leadership is founded on deeply felt experiences early in life. Youth may not be an obstacle to becoming a leader, but only if you have been through a crucible and emerged unscathed on the other side.

Most people on planet earth are living longer lives. This is due to better nutrition; improved sanitation; and the decline of diseases like smallpox, cholera, and typhoid. As longevity has increased, so too has what is accepted as the dividing line between middle age and old age—what in the modern Western world is viewed as "passed it." Two or three centuries ago, people who might today be seen as only middle aged were considered very old.

Attitudes toward the old in the rural communities of Europe's past were mixed. On the one hand they were seen as literally living proof that nature's various vicissitudes of diseases and natural disasters could be resisted. They were also seen as repositories of experience in a largely unchanging and insular world. But at the same time they were looked upon in practical terms as a burden. They didn't work but they had to be fed, unless some institution like a monastery could be made to take over the responsibility.

Grumpy old men and women

On the whole the attitude was one of respect, if grumbling respect and no one postulated serious plans for a mass culling of the old. Gradually this respectful posture toward the old shifted. Strangely, this occurred in tandem with the provision of greater governmental assistance for older people. In Great Britain, the Liberal government of David Lloyd George introduced old-age pensions in 1910. From then on the old were the recipients of various welfare payments, both directly and indirectly, as in the provision of passes offering either free or reduced tariff on public transport.

Increases in longevity combined with declines in retirement age meant that many older people could look forward to at least two decades of "retirement." But this had to be paid for by people still at work. The resentment toward the old as a group cannot be voiced even today. Therefore it often finds an outlet in humor, with older people becoming the butt of jokes; they were often shown as decrepit, dirty, and exploitative.

Older people have become conscious of their numerical strength. In the year 2000, over 60s constituted 20.7 percent of the population (the figures for Germany and Italy were 23.2 and 24.1 respectively). This led to attempts to woo these grey voters by political parties; first in West Germany in the 1980s and then in the Netherlands and Luxembourg. There have also been clear indications that older people are unhappy at being sidelined after reaching an arbitrary retirement age. This has led in legal terms to a landmark judgment in the European court. In the early 1980s, Ann Marshall, an English midwife, was unhappy with her local health authority's policy of insisting that she retire at the age of 62 (even though male colleagues could work until 65). She initiated legal proceedings which led ultimately to the European Court of Justice in Luxembourg, which found that the policy was discriminatory. The judgment found that the discrimination was based on gender; it had nothing to say about the retirement age itself.

There have been numerous European directives aiming to outlaw agism in the workforce, but these apply only to workers below the retirement age. Once they have passed the magic date they should sit back and enjoy the ride, paid for in part or in total, by the state. But many older people believe that they still have as much energy as before, and that their skills are as vital and applicable as ever. In France there has been a long-standing joke about the office worker who is asked on retirement, what he's looking forward to. "The chance to start work properly," he answers.

But even those who do not want to reenter the world of work view retirement as a time that can be filled with useful activities.

The reality is dawning that energy has little to do with age. One of the most vibrant leaders we have encountered is Sir John Parker, chairman of the UK's National Grid. His energy and flexibility mean that he works through amazing challenges together with his management team.

In many places, 60 is regarded as a magical age. (We have met owner-managers of Turkish companies who are in their mid-70s and are still working 18 hours a day.) The over 60s are better able to handle complexity. They are as good at creating strategy as their younger counterparts, but much better at getting people to buy into a strategy.

Old China

China was for many years a largely agrarian society. But even though industry and services play an ever-increasing role in the economy attitudes toward the old have remained unchanged. It's no surprise that older people should have unalloyed respect because of their age and experience. This was a central tenet of Confucian teaching, which has been translated into politics. In China, the notion of a council or board of elders is also widely respected, with the same individuals often sitting on multiple boards and sharing information for the good of all.

The Great Helmsman Mao Tse Tung was still at the pinnacle of political power at the age of 83. Zhu De remained as vice chairman of the Standing Committee of the National People's Congress until his death (aged 86). His successor, Ye Jianying, was 79 when he took on the job. Other men were considered (by Western commentators) as youngsters when they were inducted into the Politburo or Central Committee in their sixties.

It was easy to view this as a gerontocracy, a system where political power lay in the hands of the old. The same was true in Communist Russia, where the leading members of the Politburo were typically elderly men. That changed with the appointment of Mikhail Gorbachev—which ushered in the new era.

Although the age profile of China's leaders has come down to standards that wouldn't cause raised eye-brows in the West— both President Hu Jintao and Premier Wen Jiabao are in their late 60's—China is a nation and culture that still puts considerable store in experience. Experience is more than a euphemism for old. It means that those possessing it have survived the various flood-tides of recent Chinese history—the Great Leap Forward of the late 1950s, the Cultural Revolution of 1966 to 1976 and the anarchy and mayhem accompanying the actions of "The Gang of Four" during Mao's final years when various groups jockeyed, often violently, for supremacy.

During the Cultural Revolution future strongman Deng Xiaoping was banished to a tractor factory deep in the Chinese countryside; future minister for Commerce Bo Xilai (59) was imprisoned and his mother beaten to death. Those spearheading these cataclysmic events were typically young hotheads— the Red Guards. These were people whose inexperience allowed them to be carried along in the madness of loyalty to Mao's teaching. Their victims included Deng Xiaoping's son who never fully recovered from being thrown out of a fourth-floor window.

The respect for seniority is also seen in the Chinese language. Its influence stretches to wherever Chinese is spoken (and in whatever variant). When speaking with an older person, even somebody who might be only ten years older, it is customary to place *lao* in front of their surname. This is untranslatable into

English. Literally it means "old" but if this was used to translate the word the sense would be lost. In the Western world, someone addressed as, say, Old Smith or Old man Jones would probably not be flattered.

In the West, it is deprecatory, almost insulting. This meaning is entirely absent in Chinese, where *lao* not only means old but also carries with it genuine respect. When it is moved from before the surname to after it then it takes on an even greater significance. Deng Xiaoping in the last years of his life was routinely called "Deng lao," translatable into English as "Venerated Deng."

There are signs, however, that in business the attitudes to age in China are beginning to change.

China's business revolution

The UK-based *Chief Executive Officer* magazine and the Cass Business School publish an annual ranking of up-and-coming CEOs under the age of 45. The results for 2007 were revealing. The usual image of the CEO may be the grey haired, 50-something senior executive, but while the average CEO of a listed company is in their mid-50s, it is clear from the research that a new generation of younger CEOs are making their mark in the business world.[28]

China's high-flying CEOs have an average age of 47.24, compared with the 55.07 years average age of the 1,450 CEOs included in the study, and made up some 40 percent of the 160 CEOs under the age of 45.

Heading the last ranking was 37-year-old CEO, Zhengrong Ba, vice chairman and general manager of Beijing Tianhong Baoye Real Estate. The company, headquartered in Beijing, is a major player in China's burgeoning real estate business, where property prices in many of the major cities have seen double-digit growth in recent years. Ba, who graduated in real estate economics in 1990 from Renmin University of China (previously known as the People's University of China), joined the Beijing Tianhong Group shortly after graduation, becoming vice president in 1993, and CEO in 2000.

China's other representatives in the top 50 CEOs are drawn from a wide range of industries and geographies, reflecting the enormous economic growth in China across the entire business spectrum. At #3, for example, Yu Ge, 44, presides over Liaoning Cheng Da, a conglomerate based in Dalian in China's Liaoning Province, that has interests in textiles and clothing import and export, the biotech sector, and financial and commercial investment.

Japan's grey economy

As in China, age is respected in Japan, and for the same reasons. The country has some worrying statistics related to age. In the period 2000–5 life expectancy was 81.6—putting it behind only tiny Andorra in the longevity stakes. For Japanese women, the figure was 85.1.

In 2000, those over 60 constituted 23.3 percent of the total Japanese population. Japan already has the highest average age with a figure of 41.3. That is expected to increase to 53.2 by 2050. This means that attitudes toward the elderly are likely to continue to be respectful in Japan because they constitute such a sizable proportion of the population.

Traditionally, age conferred status. The firm or business where a Japanese person worked was like a second family. On joining employees were promised a job for life. The company was organized on strictly hierarchical lines, and these often mirrored seniority. Employees were also given a very clear roadmap of how they would progress within the company. The employee aged within the company, acquiring greater respect. However, all that began to unravel from the late 1980s. Lifetime employment became a dream for many, as firms abandoned their no redundancy policies, and decided to downsize. Among those affected were middle managers. The shock of losing their jobs was too much for many and led to suicides. For others, the loss of social status was something which had to be avoided, and they regularly left their homes, briefcases in hand, on the commute to nonexistent jobs, sometimes putting in the hours until their return journeys by sitting on park benches. A fortunate few found employment and an outlet for their skills, usually in much smaller companies offering far less pay.

The young Americans

The United States demonstrates many of the tensions between a brash and impatient younger generation and an older generation that keeps growing.

America traditionally has been a country for young men. The immigrant was told to "Go west, young man." The younger man would work hard, reap the reward of his toil, and then when the work of his days was over he could hope to look forward to a golden retirement, cared for by the next generation, to whom he had handed over stewardship of whatever he had created. The old were treated with respect, but it was a respect they had to earn by fading into the background.

Until comparatively recently, the experience of the older generation was valued. Stereotypes in popular entertainment like Archie Bunker would get lots of laughs, but behind it all there was an acceptance that the laughs came with a grain of wisdom.

From the 1960s there was a growing recognition that the world was changing, and many felt this was not a bad thing. Yet in the 1970s a reaction set in. In 1980 Ronald Reagan was elected president at the age of 70. But in the 1990s with the growth of information technology many younger people felt that the world really was changing, and with it the old paradigms. Experience was all very well, but it was experience earned in the old world, where information was "out there" and remote, and could not move at undreamed-of speeds along super-fine media. The world belonged to the masters of this new technology.

This was the world of the technology start-up, with founders who could become multimillionaires in a few years instead of growing their businesses. They were able to attract funding based on one-page business plans. The old timers just didn't get any of this.

But the glint of the young and the brash, versus the more subdued hues of the old was influenced by the bottom line. Older workers usually demanded better remuneration and they are not as pliable as younger inductees, who could be molded to fit the ever-changing nuances of corporate culture.

In the United States, youth is associated with energy and business dynamism. Young leaders are feted and admired. Keith Meister, head of Icahn Enterprises, is the youngest CEO in the *Fortune 1000*. Between May 31, 2007 and June 01, 2008, Meister, aged 34, delivered a return on invested capital of 52.1 percent, growing revenues by 102 percent, and outperforming many older, more experienced CEOs. In doing so, Meister proves that age is no barrier to excellent corporate performance and, increasingly, no barrier to taking up the top job in a major corporation in the United States.

Good governance

There are signs, too, that the cult of youth and age may not be mutually exclusive. The sight of the two richest Americans exchanging ideas is a powerful one. That Bill Gates, still relatively youthful, and Warren Buffett, now in his 70s, are such firm friends bodes well for the future. Gates is the erstwhile brash techie who listens to the sanguine and pragmatic Buffett.

The meeting of old and young leaders is also highlighted in the Cass research, which reveals a number of interesting findings. Unsurprisingly, of the Fortune 1000 CEOs, the majority (775) were over 50. Indeed, the average age across the whole sample was 55.43, with an age range from 34 to 85.

Taken together the various findings show a new generation of U.S. executives making CEO earlier than their predecessors and demonstrating capable performance once in the top job.

Interestingly, the youngest CEOs in the world based on average age, come from China, the emerging economic superpower, as CEO magazine's Global CEO survey in 2007 revealed. Maybe the global economy that we operate in today, and China's willingness to allow executives aged 50 and under to run major corporations has set an example that other nations, including the United States, are now beginning to follow.

Outside of China, for young CEOs at least, America fails to live up to its mantra "the land of opportunity." Surprisingly, despite the internet boom over the past 10 to 15 years, the average age of an S&P 500 CEO is 55.51. Only 24 out of 494 CEOs are age 45 or under, that is less than 5 percent, some way behind the United Kingdom, for example, with 10 percent, or Australia with 15 percent.

Looking at the average age of CEOs in the rest of the world, outside the United States and China, Australia is notable for an above average proportion of young leaders. Although only 4 CEOs from companies listed on the Australian ASX 200 index make it into the top 50, 21 out of 132 Australian ASX 200 CEOs were under the age of 45, that is 15.9 percent, significantly above the 11 percent average across all CEOs. Russia follows a similar trend.

The leaders of the future

The research highlights the willingness in China to appoint CEOs based on merit with less regard to length of service or seniority. It shows how in Japan the average age of the CEO, already significantly older than the rest of the world, is still increasing. This is symptomatic of a system of promotion which may need a radical overhaul if Japan is to restore its economic fortunes. Then there is the dearth of women CEOs of listed companies, an issue which has to be addressed.

Perhaps above all, however, the most significant fact to emerge from the research that produced this ranking is that there is no correlation between age and corporate performance. This undermines any argument that CEOs should necessarily be in their 50s and older, because of the wealth of experience they bring to the table. Not so. Talented people will succeed regardless of age, as this ranking of high-flying CEOs shows. Young CEOs can as much outperform more experienced CEOs but can just as easily fail; Nick Leeson of Bearings Bank being a case in point. For a business world in the midst of a supposed talent war, where CEO talent is, apparently, in short supply, maybe more companies should follow China's lead.

Ask Yourself

- Is age relevant to your approach to talent?
- How do you capture experience—corporate memory?
- What is your corporate narrative—do you recruit young talent and get rid of older workers?
- Where do you need age and experience in your organization? At the top? All over? In general or specialized roles?
- Can you insource age and experience—through nonexecutive directors, for instance?

Notes

1. Kroeber, A. L. and Kluckhohn, Clyde (1952) *Culture*, Meridian Books, New York.
2. We talk about cognitive therapy: the best way to change how people think is to change how they act. A change in behavior triggers a change in attitude. Culture is all about what you do. In the Western view, culture is all about the molding of attitudes, through doing and speaking. But from the Eastern perspective, culture is all about a molding of behaviors through rituals. (Actually, this is also true in the West, but the orthodoxy versus orthopraxy view means that we associate culture with how we think rather than what we do.)
3. Earley, C. P. and Peterson, Randall (2004) "The elusive cultural chameleon," *Academy of Management Learning and Education*, Vol. 3.
4. Hofstede, Geert (2001) *Culture's Consequences: Comparing Values, Behaviors, Institutions, and Organizations across Nations.* Second edition, Sage Publications; (1997) *Uncommon Sense about Organizations*, Sage; (1995) *Cultures and Organizations*, McGraw-Hill, London.
5. Brown, Tom; Crainer, Stuart; Dearlove, Des; and Rodrigues, Jorge N. (2001) *Business Minds,* FT Prentice Hall, New Jersey.
6. Ibid.
7. Trompenaars, Fons (1993) *Riding the Waves of Culture*, Nicholas Brealey, London.
8. Brake, Terence (1997) *The Global Leader*, Irwin, Chicago, IL.

9. See also Lawrence, Peter A. and Edwards, Vincent (2000) *Management in Western Europe*, Palgrave Macmillan, Basingstoke, UK.

10. Ibid.

11. Lawrence, Peter (1990) *Management in the Land of Israel*, Cheltenham, Thorens; also Baruch Yehuda, Meshoulam, Ilan, and Tzafrir, Shay (2006) "Human resource management in Israel," in Budhwar, Pawen S. and Mellhi, Kamel (eds.) *Managing Human Resource in the Middle East*, Routledge, London, pp. 180–198.

12. Crumley, Bruce (2007) "Sarkozy's bling-bling presidency," *Time,* December 20.

13. Goffee, Rob and Jones, Gareth (2006) *Why Should Anyone Be Led By You?* Harvard Business School Publishing, Boston.

14. Whorf, Benjamin Lee Science and Linguistics, Cambridge (1940) *Technology Review* (MIT), 42: pp. 229–31, 247–248.

15. http://news.bbc.co.uk/1/hi/in_depth/6405379.stm

16. Andrew P. Kakabadse, Nada K. Kakabadse, and Orhan Yavuz, (2009) "Turkish chairmen: Contrasting the art of dialogue against the discipline for governance," in Kakabadse, A. and Kakabadse, N. (eds.) *Global Boards: One Desire, Many Realities,* Palgrave Macmillan, London.

17. Adam Smith (1776) *Wealth of Nations* and (1759) *Theory of Moral Sentiments.*

18. For further information, see Ward, K., Bowman, C., and Kakabadse, A. (2005) *Designing World Class Corporate Strategies*, Elsevier/Heinemann, Oxford.

19. Definitions of diversity: There are numerous ways in which diversity has been defined. Narrow definitions tend to reflect Equal Employment Opportunity (EEO) law, and define diversity in terms of race, gender, ethnicity, age, national origin, religion, and disability. Broad definitions may include sexual/affectional orientation, values, personality characteristics, education, language, physical appearance, marital status, lifestyle, beliefs, and background characteristics such as geographic origin, tenure with the organization, and economic status. Hayles (1996), for instance, defines diversity as "All the ways in which we differ" (p. 105). He adds that the diversity concept is not limited to what people traditionally think of it as: race, gender, and disabilities (American Society for Training and Development [ASTD], 1996b)." Hayles, V. R. (1996) "Diversity training and development," in R. L. Craig (ed.) *The ASTD Training and Development Handbook*, pp. 104–123, McGraw-Hill, New York.

20. European Professional Women's Network (2008), 3rd European PWN Board Women Monitor, www.europeanpwn.net

21. Wibbeke, E. S. (2009) *Global Business Leadership*, Butterworth-Heinemann, Oxford, UK.

22. Ibid.

23. Bourne, Vanson, "A survey of 100 IT managers and CIOs in big businesses," Dimension Data, June 2008.

24. Davis, S. 'How the state is monitoring your phone', *The Week*, October 6, 2007, No. 634, p. 14.

25. In an article of 2005 in the journal *Ethics and Information Technology* (Vol. 7, No. 1, pp. 7–19), which concentrated on the new aspect of informational privacy.

26. Orwell, George (1949) *Nineteen Eighty-Four,* Secker & Warburg, London.
27. Kakabadse, N., Kakabadse, A., and Lee-Davis, L., (2008) "Smart technology: The leadership challenge," *Strategic Change*, Vol. 17, No. 2, pp. 235–249.
28. The Chief Executive Officer survey of "Fifty under fifty" is produced by Steve Coomber along with Cass Business School. It can be accessed at www.the-chiefexecutive.com. All material is used with the permission of the author.

PART III

Roll Out

Triple R Global Leader

A ready crop is a beautiful sight;
a harvested crop a source of might.

Proverb

Deliver on decisions

Communicate, tune in, understand the context and then get buy-in.
The bottom line is universal: delivery is king. Global strategy
always has a local context, an end result, a product in a customer's
hand somewhere in the world.

The Russians are coming

When the Russian company Severstal took over one of the biggest U.S. metals suppliers to Ford and General Motors, one of
its top mangers told us that the company principally negotiated
with only two bodies: the trade unions and the city mayor. It
negotiated with them to have the minimum number of redundan-
cies, to discover the best way to keep the infrastructure together,
and have the political parties support them so that the unions,
the politicians as well as the management that they inherited
would work toward improving productivity with minimum loss
to the people of the community.

The American workforce and management welcomed their
Russian owners. Productivity has increased dramatically. The
Russians together with unions are achieving enviable cost reduc-
tions in production and organisational processes rather than in
wages.

As this example demonstrates, global decisions can be followed
by fantastic local delivery. But, only if you work at it.

The art of guiding

The same principle applies at board level. A little listening and
respect goes a long way. "If you listen carefully and you've got a

finger on the pulse of the board, you can influence actions and thoughts. Plan a little ahead and talk about this. Clever, thoughtful people expect direction as long as concerns are addressed," Viscount Etienne Davignon chairman of Suez-Tractebel in Belgium told us.[1]

When we interviewed him, Viscount Davignon referred frequently to the different perspectives offered by his colleagues on the board. He was aware of and had respect for their views. Views require airing. The wisdom and experience of each member needs capturing. Showing respect for each director's independence while at the same time harnessing the range of opinions expressed into a cohesive contribution requires personal sensitivity. It also requires the clarity of mind to work toward desired outcomes.

Making things happen is what business is all about. In the final analysis, sitting around drinking rice wine is useful only if it leads to a better relationship and, as a consequence, better performance and results. Performance and results are universal goals. But, obviously, how we prefer to measure performance and results differs from situation to situation and place to place.

Delivering on decisions can never be taken for granted. Nor can it simply be bulldozed through. There is often the feeling that Western companies go through the cultural motions and then revert to cultural type once a contract is signed.

There is an important distinction to be drawn here between influencing results and driving through outcomes, which is an altogether more aggressive approach liable to create ill-feeling and discontent.

Influencing outcomes is a subtle art. An independent director of a U.S. company (who preferred to remain anonymous) expressed admiration for one chairman who knowingly influenced his colleagues to satisfy his predetermined ends. The same director also expressed his distaste for being pushed into supporting a particular decision while a member of another board. The more blatant pushing induced confrontation between the board and the chairman. In both circumstances, the intentions of the chairman were clear. The difference was the manner in which those intentions were achieved.

"He knows what he wants and he just tries to bully it through," said the director. "This is going to lead to a bust up. Not like another board on which I sit where we all know what the chairman wants, but he achieves it with style. It's a pleasure to be guided to where the chairman wanted us in the first place."

Deft delivery

Our research identified five steps toward delivering deftly on decisions:

What do people think and feel? Step 1 is the surfacing of sentiments. The global leader has to draw to the surface how people really feel about the decision, the management, and the organization; the way issues are being dealt with; and about each other as colleagues. Positions are inevitably accompanied by tense sentiments. Having drawn to the surface those powerful but hidden emotions that can undermine decisions reached, the next step is to address them.

Solve the difficult issues. Step 2 involves finding the strength to work through divisive emotions. Working through sentiments is no easy matter. Considerable resilience and discipline is needed to proceed with what is an emotionally draining experience. Needing to influence outcomes as a result of leading through change or pressing for performance improvement requires a robustness to work through tense emotions. There are no guarantees. Despite personal qualities, the individual could lose out and be forced to leave. However, not to draw out the deeply held sentiments in the team guarantees nothing will change.

Communicate and persuade. Personal resilience acts as the platform for Step 3: oratory skill. Oratory skill without strength of character is viewed as sophistry. But when force of conviction and persuasive speech are brought together, the message becomes potent. Language and tone of voice cleverly handled allow the most sensitive of conversations to take place.

Get agreement then build focus. Step 4, the focusing of the salient points in the debate. Powerful individuals enmeshed in demanding discussion can unwittingly divert the conversation down a number of unproductive avenues. One of the skills of chairing any meeting is to draw the group back to the key point of discussion.

Think ahead. Step 5, thinking several meetings ahead. Like an accomplished chess player, the effective global leader thinks several moves ahead. The world-class leader is akin to the Grand Master. He knows all the gambits and has played out the strategies many times. This involves the positioning of deliberating meetings ahead of time to mold expectations of the considerations under scrutiny. It is a way of ensuring that the leader carries people with him.

Bringing doubts into the open

In order to move from decision to delivery, people need to fully engage. The issue under debate may be contentious; the discussion uncomfortable. Yet, in order to move forward, a shared view has to be achieved. The global leader, through their skills of personal influence, guides the discussion to a point where a unanimous decision is reached.

Despite expressed commitment to the decision, senior executives often have the feeling that not all are as committed as they publicly state. Is this situation unusual? No, far from it: our research spanning many thousands of organizations indicates that these sorts of difficult and sensitive discussion are a regular although unwelcome experience for most executives, even the more seasoned ones.

Astonishingly, the level of inhibition at senior management levels is high. Thirty-six percent of top French managers to 80 percent of top Chinese managers and officials of private sector and state organizations admit to backing down from airing uncomfortable but pertinent issues. One-third of the world's organizations have senior managers who hold undeclared, but nevertheless, deeply held differences of view concerning the vision, mission, and future of the organization. In addition, approximately two-thirds of the world's top executives find it difficult to address relevant but sensitive issues.

Taking the medicine

Such was the case with a European pharmaceutical company. The newly appointed CEO concluded that the company's structure and product and services portfolio required redesign. Divestment of certain product families and less profitable subsidiaries and divisions was agreed, first with the management team and then with the board. At board discussions the management presented a united front. However, a minority felt that not only was the strategy of repositioning the firm suspect but also that members of the management team were not wholly convinced of their argument. Certain board members held private discussions with the chairman, but that led nowhere. One of the American directors, at a subsequent meeting, raised the question of rethinking the restructuring of the group, but to no avail. The chairman dampened the discussion.

Over the next few months, it became slowly evident that deep disaffection existed at senior management levels. Key business heads and support function directors were challenging the CEO at executive committee meetings. Further, two high-profile resignations led to further speculation of a divided and troubled top management. Matters came to a head when the relatively newly appointed group marketing director labeled the group's branding and pricing strategy as unrealistic. These disagreements came to the attention of board members, who, themselves, were well tuned into the organization. At the next board meeting they expressed their concerns about the leadership capacity of the CEO and also about the damage to the reputation of the organization as stories of managerial strife began to float to influential journalists. Still the chairman supported the CEO.

The underlying tensions came to the surface at a dinner the evening prior to a board meeting. The most senior of the independent directors raised the issue of damaging tensions and poor leadership. Why, the director asked, was the board not discussing reputational risk and managerial incompetence? The level of unease among the board members was evident. The chairman agreed that the senior colleague who raised the concern should canvass the opinions of the other board members. The chairman learnt that not only was the leadership of the organization a concern, but so was the chairman's tendency to suppress bad news. Greater involvement is required—was the clear message. The chairman declared surprise. The lack of trust in the CEO was nothing new; the concern about the chairman's style was.

To the chairman's credit, he did listen. To the surprise of his colleagues, he made stringent effort to adapt his leadership style. The chairman's change of style was met with admiration and positive comment. The lapses into sullen silence that had dogged previous board meetings quickly evaporated. Concerns over strategy and what was generally happening in the organization were given a full airing. More open discussion not only led to more fruitful discourse but also to genuine support for the chairman. It was agreed that the chair should explore with the CEO the strategic direction being pursued as well as the CEO's style of management. The chairman reported that the CEO remained convinced that he was on the right track and had argued his case strongly. The chairman reiterated the CEO's strategy which, within the new culture of more in-depth discussion, senior managers more readily accepted. But, concern remained over the CEO's style. Unwilling to change, the CEO left amicably to be replaced by an individual whose demeanor was favorably received by both board and management. Ironically, the same strategy is currently being pursued but with a different CEO who displays a more welcoming approach.

Is this an unusual story? Not really. In molding the future for the organization, global leaders display not only their rational, analytical side but also their philosophy and style. When concerns about strategy reach board level, suppression of either simply stores up problems for the future. Inadequate examination of either also leaves the organization vulnerable. A poorly functioning team monitors badly. Further, commitment to and ownership of any decision reached is also low. What makes things worse is that team members and top management know what is wrong and what is needed to put things right.

The tension in the way of delivery

Why do deeply held tensions arise? From our research, we identified six sources of tension in global leadership teams and some ways to overcome them.

1   Little involvement; no commitment

"I go round the board table and I ensure that everyone debates an issue," says Don Argus, chairman of BHP Billiton. "I get their views on the issue. Everyone will debate from their position of strength and from their skill strength. Now that we have everyone's position, we need to debate an outcome and give management the lead as to whether the board supports the issue or not."[2]

"The skill is reaching that desired level of commitment," adds Kelly O'Dea, chairman of Alliance HPL.[3] As O'Dea outlines, the purpose of full and frank discourse is depth of scrutiny and commitment to the decision reached.

The message is crystal clear: involve team members. But, as we have seen, many leaders fail to achieve this.

2   Lack of clarity over what everyone is contributing and when

Why is each person at the meeting table? At the time of appointment, what was the intended role and contribution of each team member? Has each contributed as expected?

These are commonplace questions which naturally induce a different response for each team member.

Drawing out the best from the team is the responsibility of the leader. One poor performing team member may be the result of a wrong appointment. Continual unsatisfactory performance and contribution is down to the leader.

Poor contributions can become a habit. A leader who is poor at drawing out the best from colleagues becomes accustomed to not being challenged. The leader and team members form a dysfunctionally comfortable relationship. The team racks up costs but offers little value. Worse still, vulnerabilities creep in undermining the organization.

3 Poorly delineated tasks

"I am doing what the rest of us as a board should be doing..." commented one director. He continued, "I am really policing the chairman, who is policing the CEO, who is being scrutinized by the shareholders, who turn to me if they cannot get anywhere. By which time, it is too late!"

If it is not clear what each and every person is doing and contributing, then decision-making will suffer. This is especially true when you are dealing with different nationalities and cultures. In China, for example, agents are widely and somewhat bewilderingly used. The potential for confusion is enormous.

4 Differences of view

Differences of view between leaders, especially when reported in the business media, raise tensions that can undermine the team. Challenge, even confrontation can be uncomfortable but tension, of itself, is no bad thing. Leaders resigning because of transparent differences of view do not bankrupt the organization and rarely damage the likelihood of delivery. The language used may be colorful and dramatic, but life goes on. One person leaving because of genuine differences of view, more often than not leads to opportunities: the opportunity to rethink and the opportunity to find a replacement and strengthen the board. Suppressed tension is the concern. If problems that should be addressed continue and remain unchallenged, they can cause irreparable harm.

5 The speed element

The biggest cultural divide often surrounds speed and timing. Speed really isn't everything.

An old Chinese parable tells how the two fastest horses began a race with the sun behind them in the east and at the end of the day inevitably found themselves facing the sun in the west. A Zen proverb says, those in a hurry do not arrive. This principle says that in matters of true learning, he who goes slow goes far. Hence, the currency of such expressions as "Haste makes waste" or "Speed is useless if you are going in the wrong direction;" Or "less haste; more speed." The trick in turning decisions into delivery is to haste slowly, to take time to absorb and assimilate information, and to shun short cuts. Patience is the key. All good things take time.

But this process needs to be led and the timescales and expectations must be continually communicated.

6   The chemistry factor

More potent than differences of view is the chemistry factor. As we have seen, chemistry is elusive but deeply important. Global leaders ask

- Can we relate?
- Can we work together?
- Do we share the same interests?
- Are we of a like mind?

Whether chemistry refers to a sharing of interests, background, experience, or values and personality, the bonding of chemistry is tested by the capacity of the parties to interpret information and events in a similar manner. Not interpreting the world in a comparable manner can be partly compensated for by friendship or what the ancient Greeks termed as *philos*, meaning deeply held friendship. If the philos dimension as well as the sharing of thinking and interpretation is lacking then it can lead to despising and disrespect—the leader's nightmare.

Unwilling to be identified, one independent director described the almost unworkable strains on her board: "I think the chief executive is great—so, too, is the chairman. But there is contempt between them. The chairman gets stuck into the CEO.

The chairman is not liked by the other board members but at least they respect his abilities. No such respect is evident from the CEO. On balance the relationship is just about workable because the chief exec tries really hard and just ignores the crap. How long this can continue, well that is another matter!"

In fact, the tension continued for another 20 months. In the intervening period, rumors of rifts were denied. The reputation of the board and the organization was slowly tarnished. The share price dropped but not dramatically. No acquisitions were pursued. To the press, media, and shareholders, the overall impression was of an organization in stagnation.

Strangely, bad chemistry sometimes evokes greater professionalism. "The chairman and I are polite to each other. We have little more to do with each other and even that is hard work," explains the CEO of one European company. "One day, I was tired, irritable, stretched in too many directions and I nearly lost my cool. I managed to keep myself restrained. Had I not that would have caused a complete breakdown in our relationship. The result would have been a catastrophe. It is just what the press and media would have wanted. The relationship cannot get better no matter how hard we both try. We are both professional. The question is: who will go first?"

The effort required to maintain a publicly respectful relationship in the full knowledge that little value is being created is considerable. The important point is that the organization should function; the leader should do his or her job; the management should get on with running the business.

What is surprising is for how long incompatible relationships continue. Some justify continuing with an apparently unworkable relationship on the board as needing to find the right time to depart. Others find the challenge of facing up to personal confrontation too daunting. Despite the recognition that one of the erring parties should go, it is, for many, emotionally easier to continue. Facing an emotionally damaging relationship is deeply discomforting, particularly when the likely response from the other party is denial.

"I have known many chairmen, CEOs and board members try to find, or create, the right time to talk things through in a professional and calm manner," says Tom Sawyer. "It rarely works. What you end up doing is using your skills and experience to keep something going that should have died ages ago. The best thing to do is make up your mind, you are going to face the situation. It's messy and uncomfortable but go through it. The relief afterwards is great."[4]

Ask Yourself

- What is the local culture regarding the use of agents and third parties?
- Do we have a united sense of purpose?
- Who are the key stakeholders?
- What do they and we care about?
- Can I handle being challenged?
- Is everyone signed up to the decision?
- Is communication constant and transparent?
- Is everyone clear on their expected contribution?
- What are the key deliverables? By when? Does everyone know?

Decide to decide

In the Anglo-American world, a decision is a decision. But else-where decision-making is about implementation. For example, in Turkey a firm would not make a decision that would increase profit in the short term but damage relationships in the long term. Understand the local dynamics of decisions.

Decisions, decisions

A decision no one buys into is dead in the organizational water. Your decisions need to be justifiable locally and globally, tactically and strategically. And, let there be no mistake, actually taking decisions lies at the heart of any leadership role. "Executives do many things in addition to making decisions. But only executives make decisions. The first managerial skill is, therefore, the making of effective decisions," Peter Drucker observed.[5] How decisions are made, and could be improved, is a topic of perennial interest to businesspeople and academics alike.

An entire academic discipline, decision science, is devoted to understanding decision-making. Much of it is built on the foundations set down by early business thinkers who believed that under a given set of circumstances human behavior was logical and therefore predictable. The fundamental belief of the likes of computer pioneer, Charles Babbage and, Scientific Management founder, Frederick Taylor, was that the decision process (and many other things) could be rationalized and systematized.[6] Based on this premise models emerged to explain the workings of commerce which, it was thought, could be extended to the way in which decisions were made.

In general, management literature defines two different types of decisions: operational decisions and strategic decisions.

Operational decisions are concerned with the day-to-day running of the business. Typical operational decisions might involve setting production levels, the decision to recruit additional employees, or to close a particular factory.

Strategic decisions are those concerned with organizational policy and direction over a longer period. So, a strategic decision might involve determining whether to enter a new market, acquire a competitor, or exit from an industry altogether.

Interestingly, the late Madan G. Singh, chair of information engineering at the Manchester Institute of Science and Technology and an acknowledged expert on decision-making, preferred an alternative breakdown of decision levels, which recognizes some of the changes taking place within companies. (Singh actually put his ideas into practice as an entrepreneur and eventually sold his business to the benefit of himself and his institution.) He divided the decision-makers in an organization into three levels of decisions:

- day-to-day decisions
- tactical decisions
- strategic decisions

Day-to-day decisions, he said, are those made by front-line staff. Collectively, they make thousands of decisions daily, most of them in a short time frame and on the basis of concrete information—answering a customer's request for information about a product, for example. Their decisions usually have a narrow scope and influence a small range of activities. Both tactical and strategic decisions, on the other hand, are longer-term decisions. The data needed to make them are much broader, extending outside the organization, and the information derived from that data is less precise, less current, and subject to more error. Tactical decisions cover a few weeks to a few months, and include decisions such as the pricing of goods and services, and deciding advertising and marketing expenditures.

Strategic decisions are those with the longest time horizon—one to five years or longer. They generally concern expanding or contracting the business or entering new geographic or product markets.

Help at hand

To help managers cope with all these decisions, there are numerous models, frameworks, tools, techniques, and software programs. One of the best-known, and most useful, is produced by Kepner-Tregoe.[7] What nearly all have in common is the assumption that business decisions are rational. Decision theory is grounded in the notion of the logical manager, and overlooks the role of intuition—or gut feel—in human decision-making. This is a very Western view of decisions. Eastern cultures take a variety of different approaches.

The *ringisei* process used by Japanese companies means that proposals circulate within the organization and are initialed by agreeing participants. This system is a manifestation of the Japanese bottom-up method of decision-making, and probably the best-known example of collectivist decision-making in business.

The traditional tendency in Japan has been to make corporate decisions from the bottom up rather than top down. The Japanese decision-making process is that of consensus building, or decision-making by consensus. Under this system, any changes in procedures and routines, tactics and even strategies are originated by those who are directly concerned with those changes. The final decision is made at the top level after an elaborate examination of the proposal through successively higher levels in the management hierarchy. The acceptance or rejection of a decision is the result of consensus at every echelon. "Ringi" (requesting a decision) is a written recommendation urging a specific course of action. The "ringi" is submitted upward to superiors and to the relevant departments until it reaches the top decision-makers. The decision-makers then pass down the decision on whether the proposal is to be finally accepted. This system enables all employees to participate in corporate policy decision-making.

When the lower or middle manager is confronted with a problem and wishes to present a solution, a meeting is called in that particular section by the section chief (*kacho*). The members of the section may agree that the idea should be pursued, but they may feel that it needs the overall support of the company. The section chief then reports this to his department head or department manager (*bucho*), and consults with him. If the department head expresses support for the section's proposal, the time-consuming activity of getting a general consensus starts.

In practice, the process of seeking a general consensus in reaching a final decision is known as "nemawashi" during which many communications and consultations are carried out repeatedly before the formal document or "ringi" is written.

The "ringi" system is used to confirm that all elements of disagreement have been eliminated at the "nemawashi" stage. It ensures that the responsibility is assumed by all the persons who have affixed their seal of approval.

In Japanese companies, the decision-making process will also often suggest the level at which a decision should be made and may even identify the person or people who should make it. Most critical of all, the process eliminates the need to "sell" the decision later. As such, it actually builds effective implementation into the decision-making process.

The analysis paralysis

Despite the growing body of evidence that many of the best business decisions are not strictly rational, the belief in decision theory persists. Indeed, most management books and ideas are inextricably linked to helping managers make logical decisions. Strategic management, for example, was a model by which strategic decisions could be made. Unfortunately, it was a model that demanded vast amounts of data. As a result, enthusiastic managers turned themselves into data addicts rather than better decision-makers. Decisions were perpetually delayed as more data were gathered in order to ensure the decision would be 100 percent certain to work. "Paralysis by analysis" became commonplace.

Many decision-making models assume that the distilled mass of experience will enable people to make accurate decisions. They enable you to learn from other peoples' experiences. Many promise the world. Feed in your particular circumstances and out will pop an answer. The danger is in concluding that the solution provided by a software package is the answer.

Whether in a software package or buried in a textbook, decision theorizing suggests that effective decision-making involves a number of logical stages. This is referred to as the "rational model of decision-making" or the "synoptic model." The latter involves a series of steps—identifying the problem; clarifying the problem; prioritizing goals; generating options; evaluating options (using appropriate analysis); comparing predicted outcomes of each option with the goals; and choosing the option which best matches the goals.

Messy reality

Alluring though they are, the trouble with such theories is that reality is often more confused and messy than a neat model can allow for. Underpinning the mathematical approach are a number of flawed assumptions—such as that decision-making is consistent; based on accurate information; free from emotion or prejudice; and rational. Another obvious drawback to any decision-making model is that identifying what you need to make a decision about is often more important than the actual decision itself. If a decision seeks to solve a problem, it may be the right decision but the wrong problem.

The reality is that managers—and especially global leaders—make decisions based on a combination of intuition, experience, and analysis. The manager in the real world does not care whether he or she is practicing an art or science. What they do care about is solving problems and reaching reliable, well-informed decisions.

This does not mean that decision theory is redundant or that decision-making models should be cast to one side. But it does mean that leaders need to be aware of their own cultural and personal biases, and develop the hardest of all decision skills—judgment.

Indeed, a number of factors mean that decision-making is becoming ever more demanding. The growth in complexity means that companies no longer encounter simple problems. And, complex decisions are now not simply the preserve of the senior-most managers but the responsibility of many others in global organizations. In addition, managers are having to deal with a flood of information—a survey by Reuters of 1,200 managers worldwide found that 43 percent thought that important decisions were delayed and their ability to make decisions affected as a result of having too much information!

These factors suggest that any techniques, models, or analytical techniques which enable managers to make more informed decisions more quickly will be in increasing demand. In the past models were the domain of economists and strategists. Now, there is increasing use of decision support systems. Some show the best types of decisions for a given situation. Typically, these involve how best to use resources. An oil refinery, for example, may use a support system to determine on a daily basis what is the optimum product that it should produce. Airlines run similar programs to establish optimum pricing levels. Other systems aim to yield increasingly better decisions based on past results. These learning-based models allow companies to take the data they have gathered and any analysis they have undertaken and gather it up in one place directly related to the decision.

There is little doubt that decision theory and the use of such models is reassuring.[8] They lend legitimacy to decisions that may be based on prejudices or hunches. But, the usefulness of decision-making models remains a leap of faith. None are foolproof, as none are universally applicable. And none can yet fully cope with the willful idiosyncrasies of human behavior.

What effective global leaders realize is that decision-making requires a subtle blend of hard data and soft contextual knowledge.

Ask Yourself

- Do we understand the difference between the decision and the decision-making process?
- What makes a decision effective?
- What is the trade-off between buy-in and speed?
- What are the grey areas and what are the nonnegotiables to your decision?
- How do we apply that locally?

Play to the politics of place

In some countries managers try to draw a sharp line between business and politics. But this is a false division. Political skills are essential to getting things done—and the bigger and more complex an organization, the bigger the need for political skills. Learn to regard compromise as a positive outcome not a failure.

The political states

In a global business world, politics—often with a capital P—lurks at every street corner. Politics and business have never been more closely intertwined. Let's first look at how politics at a national level can impact on the business world—and vice versa. It is not our intention to pick on America, but few countries illustrate the point better.

It says a lot about leadership, for instance, that the election of Barack Obama as its president has had a profound effect on how people around the world perceive America.

It is no secret that if they had had a vote in the previous U.S. presidential election most Europeans would not have cast it for George W. Bush. Across the Atlantic, the former president was commonly viewed with great suspicion. "Under the previous administration I always needed to be ready to respond to questions about the American people electing Bush, to defuse their frustrations about that, and create an atmosphere that shows I was sensitive to their bewilderment and perhaps even make a few jokes myself about how and why the US was at an all-time low in terms of general popularity," notes Allyson Stewart-Allen, a London-based American consultant and co-author of *Working with Americans.*[9]

Increasingly it is clear that how people feel about a leader goes beyond the personal. European dislike for American involvement in the Iraq War, for example, was taken out on American companies and brands.

It started with the decision to go to war. This sparked immediate knee-jerk boycotting of American companies and products. A Hamburg restaurant chain refused to sell Budweiser or Marlboro. In Bayonne, France the staff of one bar poured its entire stock of Coca-Cola down the drain. Mecca Cola was launched by a French entrepreneur under the slogan "No more drinking stupid, drink with commitment."

The scapegoats were—and are—predictable. McDonald's, Starbucks, Marlboro, Levi's, and so on are the quintessential American brands. For those in doubt, the website www.consumers-against-war.de carried a blacklist of 25 U.S. companies for German consumers to avoid. Others, too, suffered. The long-legged and long-lived doll, Barbie, for example, is viewed as all-American. One-third of respondents to a survey of international consumers by GMI, a Seattle-based market research company, said they would avoid purchasing the shapely doll because of her American origins. Across the board 20 percent of the 8,000 international consumers surveyed said they would avoid U.S. companies and products.

While the boycotts were never wholehearted, sporadic skirmishes rather than outright war, their longer-term impact is now becoming clear. Distrust lingers. American companies have and are suffering commercially. Mecca Cola may not have shaken Coca-Cola to its roots but it quickly recorded annual sales of 3.6 million euros in France alone. At the beginning of 2004 the Washington-based research group, the Institute for Research: Middle Eastern Policy, estimated that anti-Americanism was costing U.S. companies some $9.4 billion a year in lost revenue.

The problem for many leading U.S. companies is that their brand positioning is inextricably linked with their country of origin. Brands such as Levis, Nike, and American Express are built on their American heritage. They appeal to consumers attracted by the American way of life. Indeed, since 1945, being American has generally been seen as cool. If that is no longer the case then the damage to U.S. brands could be significant. Eight of the world's top 10 brands—Coca-Cola, Microsoft, IBM, GE, Intel, Disney, McDonald's, and Marlboro—are American.

Of course, Americans have also boycotted products from other countries. Remember Freedom Fries?

Here to stay?

The first and most important question must be whether the consumer backlash is likely to prove long lasting or slowly disappear. As Barack Obama begins his first term, Americans on the ground in Europe—and those responsible for them being there—are contemplating whether longer-term attitudes and behaviors have been affected. There is no doubt that the election of the first black president has boosted America's image in many parts of the world. Yet, memories of Bush linger. The question is how will these affect American businesses and brands? How significant are the politics of place?

Opinions differ. Research in 2003 by Harvard Business School Professor John Quelch and assistant professor Douglas Holt found that any ill-feeling toward the United States was soon forgotten—especially when it came to fast food and soft drinks. Of 1,800 consumers surveyed globally from 12 countries, such as Egypt, Turkey, and Indonesia, approximately 88 percent selected famous global brands over local alternatives. "It appears that consumer interest in new brands was short-lived, and they have reverted to trusted global products," concludes Professor Quelch.

Another poll conducted shortly afterwards, however, suggests that attitudes on the ground were still polarized. The Global Market Insite (GMI) WorldPoll was carried out in the wake of President Bush's November 2004 reelection. If the response of the German consumers is indicative of general feeling in Europe then U.S. companies should be concerned. Fifty-six percent named U.S. motor giant General Motors as a key American brand. Forty-two percent said that they would not purchase one of the company's vehicles.

Storms tend to blow over. However, many of the issues raised—such as skepticism about the dominance of big American brands—are long standing and will not disappear. They will have to be tackled at some point. More recently, too, other U.S. companies have found themselves in the dock of public opinion, Nike for using sweatshops, eBay for selling Nazi memorabilia, and Google for its stance on data protection in China.

Sense and sensitivity

Of course, it isn't just American companies that are affected by the politics of place. Shell has come under increasing pressure over its activities in Nigeria; and BP found itself pilloried by Green Peace over its attempts to dispose of the Brent Spar oil storage facility in the early 1990s. There will be many other examples in future.

So what can and should global business leaders do? They could choose to wrap themselves in their national flag and brazen it out. This may be tempting, but in the case of American companies would simply confirm the stereotype. It is not a popular option. Indeed, American business leaders now often carefully distance themselves from their American roots. This can mean paying attention to apparently unimportant issues such as your appearance. One American executive who regularly travels to Europe quips that she leaves her Stars and Stripes ear rings at home these days.

On the ground most of the Americans in Europe we talk to have little time for gung-ho nationalism as a way forward. Indeed, their approach is almost universally the same: tread carefully and tune in to cultural differences more keenly than ever before.

Only connect

Two things lie at the heart of cultural awareness: acceptance of just how different cultures can be and communication. What links them is an openness of mind and generosity of spirit.

The cultural divide should not be underestimated. Think heterogeneous. The differences can be basic. Research by the academics Albert Alesina, Rafael Di Tella, and Robert MacCulloch analyzed the different attitudes to the notion of "happiness" of Americans and Europeans. The trio studied 128,000 survey responses and found that inequality—perceived or real—had a significant negative effect on happiness in Europe but not in the United States. The conclusion is that Europeans prefer more equal societies. Americans, on the other hand, are happier to live alongside inequality. Their view is that, in their socially mobile society, the deprived have a realistic chance of making their lives better.

The second issue is communication. Gary Kuusisto, who went back to the United States after a three-year stint as European Director of Learning at Gillette recounts

> I realized the meeting was in trouble when my American colleague opened the workshop by saying to our European delegates, 'Glue your hair down, and hang on to your seats.' I could tell by the pained glances I was receiving from the audience that what was intended to be a relaxed, informal greeting had turned the atmosphere to gloom. The Europeans, whose English skills were excellent, were thinking this would be two days of struggling to translate. The American was wondering why no one was participating. As an American, who has lived and worked in Europe, I soon realized the importance of using clear, non-colloquial English. The cost of 'lost in translation' is too high. By the way, what he meant to say was, 'Let us begin'.

Richard Pooley of the communication firm, Canning says

> Not only do American business people need to learn to read between the lines of what their European partners are saying, they need to adapt the way they speak their own language. Great if they can speak Spanish, French or German. But English is pretty well accepted as the lingua franca of business. However Americans—and the British—cause a lot of misunderstanding and resentment by dominating business

discussion with fast-paced, colloquial English. Ask more questions, listen, give non-native English speakers time to speak ... and the image of the overbearing and arrogant American will fast disappear.

Improving communication may also involve changing corporate structures so that Americans do not necessarily run European subsidiaries. This is already happening according to Bob Gogel, an experienced CEO and the editor of *Chief European Officer*, a book exploring the role of managers in the European operations of U.S. multinationals. "The days of sending hordes of American managers to run European activities are gone," says Gogel, American but France-based. "Companies now require executive talent that is both far more business savvy than in the past and ultra-sensitive to every cultural nuance."

For all this there is some good news. As Allyson Stewart-Allen puts it: "The appetite to make money from Americans and in America seems undiminished."

Small 'p's

The big issue behind all of this is politics—with as big a P as you wish and depending on the circumstances. Positioning ideas so that others become more receptive, using personal charm in order to persuade others and thinking about meetings and situations ahead are the elements of influencing for favorable outcomes. For the less than accomplished player, adopting the very same tactics comes over as manipulative and overly political. Influencing in order to achieve particular outcomes in diverse and complex circumstances requires thought, sensitivity, and sincerity. Being conscious of the reactions of others and adjusting style and approach in order to accommodate personalities is fundamental to the process of influence. Such effort should be undertaken in the best interests of the management and the organization.

Politics is about influencing people. Power is an organizational lever. But, let us draw an important distinction: you can be politically successful without power. One can be all powerful and a political failure. In the long run, good politics is usually more effective than raw power.

In the West, politics with a small p has a bad name. But in the East, there is a recognition that political skills are essential to getting things done—and the bigger and more complex an organization is, the bigger the need for political skills. Compromise is a positive outcome not a failure. Calling someone a political operator in China is a great compliment.

Remembering the Prince

In some countries managers try to draw a sharp line between business and politics. But this is a false division. In most countries, managers recognize that the lines are blurred. Nonmarket strategy is the norm.

Politics are facts of corporate life, and there's no doubt as to their patron saint: the Florentine diplomat and author Niccolò Machiavelli. Machiavelli's bible on power is *The Prince*.[10] Within it, embedded beneath details of Alexander VI's tribulations, lie a ready supply of aphorisms and insights which are, perhaps sadly, as appropriate to many of today's managers and organizations as they were half a millennium ago.

Machiavelli portrayed a world of cunning and often brutal opportunism. "I believe also that he will be successful who directs his actions according to the spirit of the time, and that he whose actions do not accord with the time will not be successful," he wrote.

Machiavelli gave advice on managing change and sustaining motivation, and even had advice for executives acquiring companies in other countries: "But when states are acquired in a country differing in language, customs, or laws, there are difficulties, and good fortune and great energy are needed to hold them, and one of the greatest and most real helps would be that he who has acquired them should go and reside there ... Because if one is on the spot, disorders are seen as they spring up, and one can quickly remedy them; but if one is not at hand, they are heard of only when they are great, and then one can no longer remedy them." Executives throughout the world will be able to identify with Machiavelli's analysis.

Unfortunately, Machiavelli's brand of politics—where the end justifies the means—means that his name has become synonymous with the classic scheming and unprincipled villain. It has also helped give politics a bad name. (Although the countless badly behaved politicians over the years have probably done more in this regard).

In reality, however, politics is about a process of negotiation between different vested interests to reach a settlement. The only alternative is war. Politics then is a necessary part of organizational and social life. When those vested interests are magnified by a myriad of local issues and attitudes, politics becomes even more vital. That is why political skills are so important to the global business leader.

Ask Yourself

- How do you understand organizational politics?
- Why is the political process so important?
- How can you remove the negative connotations?
- How do you influence events and decisions?
- How equipped are you to handle the political process?

Treat people fairly

This point may seem somewhat incongruous with the previous point, But, in reality, it explains why using politics rather than power is more effective. The need to feel treated fairly is universal. Across the world, people will work very long hours and be content if they feel they are treated fairly and respectfully.

Fair world

We worked with a German company. It had subsidiaries around the world. Its executives in the United States were paid more than the German CEO of the entire organization. This discrepancy between salaries became a big issue. It was decided to get it out into the open. It took six months of preparation getting people onside and explaining the cultural and commercial reasons why, for example, the marketing director in Japan was paid much the same as the group CEO. The meeting took seven hours.

The result was the realization and appreciation that the German executives had to accept local realities. They had to accept that their Japanese colleagues were paid a little more than them and that their American colleagues were paid much more. In the end everyone bought into this reality. They knew that the cohesion of the company was more important than local salary expectations.

One of the universal truths is that people expect and deserve to be treated fairly. You can be sure if someone is treated unfairly then the news will spread like wildfire around the organization.

While the need for fairness and understanding of the concept is universal, fairness has to be managed in a local context. What is fair in Belgium may be construed differently in Singapore.

Renée Mauborgne and Chan Kim, authors of *Blue Ocean Strategy*, talk of the concept of Fair Process. "Transformation requires that companies earn the intellectual and emotional commitment of their employees. To do so requires a degree of fairness in making and executing decisions. All a company's plans will come to nothing if they are not supported by employees. Fair process is based on the simple human need for intellectual and emotional recognition. Without fair process it can be difficult for companies even to achieve something their people generally support," say Kim and Mauborgne.

They argue that companies first need to ask whether they engage people in decisions that affect them. "Do they ask for input and allow people to refute the merit of one another's ideas? Do they explain why decisions are made and why some opinions have been overridden? And, after a decision is made, are the rules clearly stated so that people understand the new standards, the targets, responsibilities and penalties?"[11]

There is, as always, a balance to be struck. One person's notion of fairness is not necessarily the same as a colleague's in another context. It is the leader's job to establish certain guidelines and standards. It is often the case in a global organization that local managers do not behave fairly according to other views because of local traditions. In such cases, the workforce and community look to top management to supervise and control so that undesired local practices are removed. For example, nepotism is something only top management can deal with.

The paradox is an enormously challenging one. Leaders must live by the stated values of the company, irrespective of context. Yet they must be culturally and contextually sensitive while being consistent to certain principles.

It's a people thing

The roots of fairness usually lie in a shared sense of purpose and direction. One of our interviewees was Major General Steve Rippe, executive vice president of the Protestant Episcopal Cathedral Foundation in Washington DC. He said of his relationship with his Bishop: "I'm very close to the Bishop. We both hold a philosophy of grass roots, decentralize, get close to the people. We have supported each other throughout this change process. It has been a memorable experience and very fulfilling."[12]

As shown in Shot #15, chemistry is built on a similar interpretation of events, personal affinity, and group membership. Being part of a team requires wholeheartedly accepting the responsibility of membership of the team—and being committed to certain shared beliefs.

Such deep sentiments are commonly termed values—what each person truly values. Certain individuals predominantly value outcomes. They are driven by tangible results. Whether they like or dislike others is totally immaterial—friend or no friend can you do the job? Others more value conduct, ways of speaking, and doing. Certain people may consider it rude to swear and on hearing a term of abuse, irrespective of how it was intended, find it difficult to listen and respect the other party's point of view. Thus, two individuals theoretically suited to work together because they share similar experiences or industry knowledge may find it in practice difficult to tolerate each other's presence. The manner by which they address each other causes tension, irrespective of the topic of conversation.

The mix and match of values determines each person's approach to task and goal completion as well as their leadership style. People carry their values on the sleeve. The value predispositions of the person are evident to others. How they think and feel, strongly determines the manner of response of others. Of course, the skill is to be conscious of one's own value orientation and how that influences others. Such sensitivity and awareness is deeply appreciated and profoundly and positively shapes the morale and motivation of those around.

Ask Yourself

- How do you understand the concept of fairness?

- Is it a universal truth that all people want to be treated fairly?
- How can you ensure that you treat people with respect?
- How do the people who work with you and for you understand fairness?
- What are the core principles of you and your organization?

Learn as you go

In the West, companies associate management development with being sent on external training programs. But elsewhere development happens more naturally in the workplace through mentoring and other informal coaching processes. In developing countries, external programs are valued as an additional opportunity. For any global leader willingness to learn is crucial.

Learnability

The Indian company Infosys talks about *learnability*—the ability of an individual to derive generic learning from specific situations and apply them to a new unstructured situation. Infosys has realized that the world is changing so quickly—and will continue to do so—that hiring people who are comfortable being narrow functional specialists with frozen knowledge is not the way forward. It wants people who are willing to learn—always.

Learning starts on day one. New Infosys recruits spend time at its huge educational complex in Mysore where there are 200 faculty, and room for up to 11,000 employees at a time. They have 16 weeks of training in technical and soft skills.

What is particularly interesting about Infosys is how it has seized the agenda. It sends its best young people to Harvard as a statement of its intent. Think of the status this bestows on young Indians working with the company. Being given the opportunity to learn more at one of the great universities of the world is the ultimate incentive. How many Western companies attach learning to status and incentives so closely or so powerfully?

Infosys brings in bright people from outside India. It launched an internship program in 2000 to attract students from the world's leading business schools. Some 275 students from Harvard, Stanford, and others now spend a summer working at Infosys. In addition, Infosys has a series of projects in collaboration with 300 universities in India and overseas designed to increase interest in Infosys among undergraduates, and to help gear course curricula toward its needs.

Learning to compete

Learning is at the forefront of the reinvention of India and China in recent years.

In India, for example, there are more than 1,000 home-grown MBA courses. Among them is the Indian School of Business (ISB) which offers a one-year MBA and, of which, Don Jacobs, dean emeritus of the Kellogg School has said: "It's unlikely that we will see more than one other business school of the scale of the ISB launched in our lifetime."

The roots of business education in India are longer established than might be assumed. The Indian Institute of Management in Ahmedabad was set up in 1961 helped by support from Harvard Business School faculty. But, with a reservoir of potential faculty, a fast-moving business sector and growing power in the world economy, Indian business schools are only now coming of age.

The repercussions of the rise in the quality and quantity of Indian business education are—and will be—felt elsewhere. First, it is clear that the flow of knowledge has changed. The assumption in the past was that other emerging markets could learn from India. Now, the flow of knowledge is two-way; it is recognized that Western companies and executives also can learn from India.

"India is an extremely interesting laboratory right now," says Gita Piramal, editor of *The Smart Manager*, one of India's leading business magazines. "Customers do not know how to be customers, and hence react in completely unexpected ways. Managers in India have to be able to deal with the unexpected and be flexible to a far greater degree than in developed countries."

Learning Chinese

A similar thirst for education can be found in China. While the business book market is becalmed in the Western world, in China it is fast expanding as young executives seek out new skills and insights. Western management gurus are now regular visitors to China's major cities.

China is also home to a growing number of business schools offering Western-style business education. Rutgers University and Michigan Business School are among the Western business schools with a presence in China. Training companies are also moving into the country—the Covey Leadership Center, Achieve Global, and Training Solutions all have Chinese operations. Little wonder: China is expected to be the largest market for management education in the next two decades.

Research by a British-based academic, Harold Chee of the UK business school Ashridge, suggests that translating theory into practice remains elusive. Chee interviewed Chinese managers who had been through some form of Western-style management training. The managers recognized the usefulness of much of what they learned. But, on returning to work they found it difficult to apply.

The reasons were partly cultural. Respect for older managers makes younger managers reluctant to challenge traditional ideas. Political correctness is sometimes seen as more important than organizational effectiveness. In addition, some things taken for granted in the West—data about customers for example—are simply unavailable. Even if you have read Kotler on marketing, try marketing without data.

The reality is that exporting Western management en masse simply won't work. Many Western management techniques rest uneasily with the Chinese culture. Business in China is still centered around relationships and contacts, what the Chinese call *guanxi*. This makes them more open to some ideas than others.

Learning to learn

As learning becomes increasingly recognized as a key competitive weapon, the challenge for leaders is to better understand how they themselves learn and to consider how they create learning opportunities for others in their team.

Context is king, but there's a wrinkle: Intimacy of understanding of the other is not just about gauging their reactions but about appreciating their style of learning.

Some learn through concepts. They are quick. Give them an idea and the benefits or disadvantages are quickly assessed and a conclusion reached. Such individuals are analytical in the way they structure their argument.

Others learn through experience. Pragmatically inclined, such an individual needs to touch and feel the situation. Little learning takes place until the individual has been immersed in the project. However, more down-to-earth learning takes time in order to fully appreciate the nature of the challenges being faced. People who learn from experience may pride themselves that they are strategic and future thinking oriented, but in reality they are not. Until a situation hits them in the face they do not fully appreciate what they face.

Still others learn from their interactions with people. Ambience; depth of relationship; warmth of conversation: these are all important ingredients for the learning process. For those analytically inclined, such learning is regarded as too emotional. In contrast, those that thrive on relationships, analytically driven judgment devoid of immersion in context is too cold, unfeeling, and possibly out of touch. How can a meaningful decision be reached if there is little appreciation of how management, staff, and other stakeholders feel and will react? Without others owning decisions, no progress is made. For the feelings oriented learner, sterile meetings lapse into debating societies: endless chatter, no substance.

There still remains a fourth group. A relatively small minority of people learn through pain. Tell them; show them; confront them; and still nothing goes in. Not until that person is hurt and experiences the trauma of not changing, little happens. The question remains, how much pain and for how long does the individual resist before they learn?

Thinking meetings ahead is as much about the positioning of issues as it is about assessing the response of others. Appreciating colleagues' styles of learning and the level of incubation required before an idea hatches requires an awareness of the timescales involved.

What matters is that the leader recognizes his and others' style of learning and does not unthinkingly assume that his/her approach is that of others. "I read others as they are, not how I would like them to be," concludes James Parkel, president of the American Association of Retired Persons.[13]

Multiple insights

Particularly worth considering are the insights of Howard Gardner, the John H. and Elisabeth A. Hobbs professor of cognition and education at the Harvard Graduate School of Education, and adjunct professor of psychology at Harvard University.

Moving on from his work on multiple intelligence, Gardner is now focusing on the future and "the cognitive abilities that will command a premium in the years ahead." In the new technological and information age, he offers an insight into the qualities of thinking that will allow people to survive and prosper in the twenty-first century, both in work and life generally.

Gardner identifies five ways of thinking that will be even more important in the future. These he labels, the disciplined mind, the synthesizing mind, the creating mind, the respectful mind, and the ethical mind.

In conversation with our colleague Des Dearlove, Gardner explained the different minds:

"The disciplined mind is knowing something very well, being an expert in an art, or craft, or profession and keeping it up. That means being disciplined. If you don't have a disciplined mind, you really don't have a job at all, or you end up working for somebody who does."

"The synthesizing mind stems from the fact that we all are deluged with information. How do you decide what to pay attention to, what to ignore, how to put it together in a way that makes sense to you? How do you communicate your synthesis to other people?"

"The third kind of mind, the creating mind, is basically coming up with something new that eventually affects how other people are and think. If it is 'thinking outside the box' then the disciplined and synthesizing minds provide the box and, for many people, that's enough and you wouldn't want everybody to be creative or the world would be too chaotic. But for some cutting edge or eccentric few, it's thinking and doing stuff that really ends up affecting a lot of other people."

"The respectful mind is very simple, and certainly goes back to pre-biblical, pre-literate times. Basically it means giving other people the benefit of the doubt, trying to know them, trying to understand them, not being too judgemental and being capable of forgiveness."

"It begins at birth. Infants notice how other people treat one another and how they treat themselves. The reason it's so acutely important nowadays is because of the diverse society we live in. My belief in the importance of the respectful mind has caused me to change my views about issues like whether women students in France should be allowed to wear the hijab."

"The last mind, the ethical mind, is one that I've been working on intensively for a decade plus. The ethical mind is a mind that is capable of abstraction. And the ethical mind basically can think about oneself abstracting. So I'm not just Howard Gardner, but I'm Howard Gardner who is a journalist, an author, a lawyer, an engineer, whatever. I have a role occupationally and I'm also a citizen; I'm a citizen of my community, my city, my state, my region, my nation, the world. The ethical mind asks, what are my responsibilities as a journalist, what are my responsibilities as a citizen of London, the UK, of the planet?"

"Individuals involved in management need to think about their own minds, and the extent to which those minds embody discipline, synthesizing capacity, creativity, respect and ethics. If they are lacking on these dimensions, what might they do to enhance them? How should they assemble teams, and can one person's strength compensate for the weaknesses of others?"[14]

Gardner's insights are vitally important for all involved in global business. They provide a poignant and stretching challenge to each of us. Are we willing to learn?

Ask Yourself

- Why do organizations struggle to develop their people?
- How can you ensure that the individuals who make up your organization are open to new ideas and learning?
- How do you handle those who thrive on learning through pain?
- How can you think about development in a more productive way?
- How do you ensure you recruit people committed to learning?
- How do you give people opportunities to learn?
- How do you learn most?
- How can you learn more?

Question authority

In the West, people don't challenge authority for fear of appearing incompetent and losing their jobs. In the East, they don't challenge authority because they don't want to upset the "harmony." Yet, too much harmony can be as oppressive—and ineffective—as too much conflict.

Questioning questions

Accepting things as they are is not leadership. Achieving change inevitably involves questioning the orthodoxy, quizzing individuals, challenging long-held assumptions.

The assumption is that Eastern cultures don't question authority. This isn't necessarily true. We have been to a Chinese company where a room full of factory workers—all women—were more than happy to question and constructively criticize their male boss. Why? Because their questioning was based on efficiency and effectiveness rather than the boss's performance.

As with so many other topics we have discussed, the leader sets the climate. If the style of the leader is to be open and transparent then that percolates down. Constructive criticism is infectious.

This is something we have encountered in our work with the boards of Turkish companies. In Turkey meetings are lively, engaging, formal as well as informal. Leaders emphasize the flexibility and friendliness of communication partly determined by their interconnectedness. "We know each other well. That helps a great deal. It is our personal knowledge of each other and respect for each other that helps us sort out our problems," one Turkish leader told us.

In contrast, we have worked with boards in the United States and United Kingdom where a lack of intimacy with each other discourages open contribution. In order to mitigate the risk of social exclusion from the group if stressful or conflicting information is introduced, Western board members can suppress information and ideas in favor of conformity. Ambiguous or complex information tends to be dismissed as unmanageable. The plague of Anglo-American boards of not addressing known concerns occurs less on Turkish boards, where major issues are often addressed outside, if within meetings proves to be too challenging.

Nothing is personal

Examination of any proposal requires the challenging of assumptions and a critique of the logic and consistency of the argument presented. In the heat of discussion, standing back and recognizing the benefits to be gained from stretching analysis not only requires a sharp and logical mind, but also a personal quality to not take offence and instinctively assume that critique is a cover for personally directed criticism.

Leadership is about asking questions, providing an alternative view, being a skeptical voice when all are in agreement. It is the leader's job to create a culture of constructive dialog; to interrogate the argument; to provide intellectual due diligence; to push and question in search of the best solution.

Aside from ensuring the success of the proposal, reducing risk, and safeguarding the reputation of the organization, one additional and powerful benefit from interrogating the argument is commitment. A robust management putting forward a well-prepared case, which is analyzed in a systematic and logical manner, not only strengthens the case but encourages greater commitment from those involved. Working together to improve proposals enables all concerned to identify with the outcome as well as allowing recognition of each other's strengths and contribution. Well-positioned logic and constructive criticism strengthen relationships, rather than damaging them.

In his mid-30s, Vadim Makhov is chairman and has been chairman of companies as well as former head of strategy for the Severstal Group, the Russian steel giant. He speaks perfect Russian, English, and French, and is adept at dealing with individuals and groups. Friendly, warm, and always polite, Makhov exudes a confidence that encourages board members and management to speak their mind. "I use myself as the example," Makhov says. "I always question but never hurt. I explore but never put anyone down. As chairman of the board, my job is to create a context and a set of practices that allows members of the board to get to the heart of the case but emerge as friends."[15]

No one is saying this is an easy task; far from it. It is actually one of the hardest skills for a leader to master. It is also one of the areas where the chairman requires different skills to the CEO. To some extent, CEOs can rely on bombast to interrogate a case. The effective leader uses a more subtle, nuanced style. The job of the CEO requires them to ask the right questions of their reports. The job of the leader is to create the environment and context in which the right questions are asked by others. Simply put, a leader who behaves as grand inquisitor is likely to be isolated from the executive team, and unable to provide a sounding board to test ideas.

Encouraging criticism requires resilience and robustness. Resilience is needed to respond positively to comment, even if critical, and recognize that the contribution is worthwhile. Such resilience is essential in order to gain from the debate. This requires the leader to build and maintain robust relationships.

Debates can be lively and seemingly personal. "Nothing is personal and should not be taken as such. Many have the intellect, but not the personal stamina for the heat of discussion!" advises Vadim Makhov.[16]

The art of challenging

The first step in challenging is to break down the argument into workable components.

Aclan Acar, experienced banker and CEO of Dogus Otomotiv, described, when as CEO of Turkey's Ottoman Bank he took steps to improve the risk management capability of the organization. A proposal was submitted, together with external providers, to develop the risk management systems of Ottoman Bank. "We needed risk management qualities on the board," recalls Aclan Acar. "We got a proposal from them. They designed a risk management system for the bank, which covered market risk, operational risk, credit risk and so on. We were far ahead of what government did."[17]

The quality of the submission was evident. The ensuing scrutiny of the proposal and its acceptance and implementation led to the appointment of an additional board member whose prime responsibility was risk management and assessment.

Thus, in breaking down the proposal, the first question is, what is the value to the organization? Before a detailed examination of the case proceeds, the value-to-whom consideration requires scrutiny. A good idea which contributes little to the enhancement of the organization is not worthy of further attention.

The second step is to position the argument. The leader determines the quality of discussion in verbalizing the argument. They foster dialog and discussion. Dialog encourages in-depth, uninhibited exploration, whereas debate induces win/lose, the taking of sides, for and against, so that the most powerful presence in the room carries the case, irrespective of whether that is the best argument.

The third step is to manage expectations. This involves positioning the argument and preparing the management team. Remember, too, that no one likes surprises.

The fourth step is to have a full and frank discussion. Exactly what full and frank means will depend on the individual situation. A team made up of people who know each other well may be more or less polite in how they discuss the issues, but discuss them all teams must.

The fifth step is to rework the argument. Sound discussion is provided if expectations have been appropriately positioned.

Once the interrogation has run its course and further work is necessary from the management team, practical steps to reworking the argument and winning final approval add a final sense of completion.

Commitment through questioning

It should never be forgotten that the purpose of questioning is to build commitment. "I always ask, are you committed to this project and do you have the team really behind you?" says David Clarke former chairman of Macquarie Bank.[18] "No matter how well thought through is the case put before the board, the commitment to turn ideas into action needs to be evident."

For some, interrogating the argument is uncomfortable. Critique is taken as personal criticism, more likely so by the champion of a project. In fact, well handled, the converse is true. Critique not only strengthens the argument, it attracts greater involvement. The more individuals have dug deep, the greater the likelihood of commitment, especially when the going gets tough.

Many leaders use the term debate to describe the intensity of the conversation. Some of those we have met prefer an alternative view.

"You should understand people. You make sure that all basic opinions are taken into account. Everyone around the table learns. Through real sharing of opinion, people better understand and communicate well," Vadim Makhov told us.[19]

This alternative view is captured in the term dialog. Vadim Makhov makes reference to dialog, not debate. While the terms are sometimes used interchangeably, in fact the difference between them is considerable.

Dialog goes back to ancient Greece. It is incredible to think that Socrates, one of the most famous philosophers, orators, teachers, and intellectuals of his day, did not write anything. Plato wrote about Socrates, who was his mentor. What we have is Socrates, second hand. Socrates championed dialog, not debate, for the purposes of achieving diligent inquiry. Socrates' unique contribution to the art of rhetoric is about reasoning, the construction of an argument and refutation of argument being a collaborative rather than an adversarial experience. In Socratic dialog, no one wins or loses, but all are engaged. The search is for the very best argument.

What is the best supportive case? What are the very best of objections? As Vadim Makhov emphasizes learning has to totally encompass the individual and the group, the essence of Socratic philosophy.

The term dialog comes from two Greek roots, *dia*, meaning flowing through and *logo* meaning the clarifying of assumptions and mental modes. The emphasis is on continuous conversation which can involve negotiation, compromise, mutual exploration, inquiry, with the cycle repeating itself many times over. (There are echoes here of Japanese Total Quality.)

Sounds simple enough, but not according to Socrates. For Socrates dialog is a state of mind, not a mode of conversation. Such state of mind is not easily realized.

More common is debate, a particularly English innovation captured in the very structure of the House of Commons, the lower chamber of the UK's Houses of Parliament. Debate denotes beating down, breaking the argument of the other side. Debate requires taking sides and confrontation. The side that wins, wins the argument. Winning and not necessarily emerging with the best case distinguishes debate from dialog. Winning can be based on strength of argument. Winning can also be entirely dependent on undermining the case of the other side, worst still, discrediting the other side, rather than paying attention to improving one's own case. Debate could also mean bullying. The loudest voice wins irrespective of the prevailing logic.

In the business world understanding the difference between debate and dialog is vital if the arguments put forward are to be truly interrogated, understood, and acted on. The global leader favors dialog—but understands that it is not for the faint-hearted.

Ask Yourself

- What prevents people from speaking up?
- How can you mitigate these fears?
- Is speaking up the way to question authority?
- What is the relevance of a proposition to the organization and its strategy and policies?
- How well is the case aligned with other initiatives being pursued?
- What is the commitment of management to the initiative?
- What quality of evidence supports the case?
- How well sequenced is the argument justifying the case?
- Is your quality of dialog driven by addressing issues and challenges or by who sits in the room with you?

Understand who carries the can

Blame is not universal. Different cultures allocate responsibility very differently when things go wrong. Understanding these differences—and what's at stake for the organization and the individual—helps the global leader make sense of abstract notions such as risk-taking and stress in different parts of the world.

Stress factors

Stress means different things in different places. In the Western world it tends to be associated with being in demand and under pressure. But in Russia and China, it means being out of favor. So, in Russia, for instance, stress may be associated with a demotion. We met one Russian manager who used to report directly to one of the country's oligarchs, but over time he started reporting to the HR director. Although his responsibilities and remuneration remained the same, he found the experience very stressful due to reporting to a less senior boss. In China, too, stress results from losing face. The same is true in Japan.

A few years ago we were told that Sony made the perfectly sensible decision to reduce the number of board members from an unwieldy 27 (typical of a Japanese board) to a more workable 11 (typical of the U.S. model). The problem, of course, was that this meant that 16 senior managers would no longer have a seat on the board. For Japanese managers, this represented a hugely stressful loss of status. But, as bad as it was for the managers, it was much worse for their wives for whom the status of their husbands confers special privileges in the community including preferential treatment at clubs and restaurants. This made it necessary for the chairman of the company to write to each wife and explain personally that this demotion was no disgrace, otherwise they might divorce their husbands. One of the authors (Andrew) met the unfortunate letter writer several years later and he explained that it was one of the most difficult and stress inducing tasks of his long and distinguished career.

Blame games

Dealing with blame—how it's apportioned, whether it is taken on the chin or passed on to others—is an essential, though over-looked element of culture. It's also very important in any discussion of the relationship between business and culture.

What happens when things go wrong? This may be the decline into bankruptcy of a once strong corporation, or carelessness and negligence in dealing with the general public's health causing a mass product recall.

Societies in Western Europe (especially the British Isles), and North America are individualistic; they place great importance on the role and responsibilities of the individual. But when it comes to dealing with blame these societies show a remarkable shift away from the individual and toward the collective. There are ideals like the Anglo-Saxon notion of "Taking it on the chin" or the American "Taking one for the team," but practice often falls short. In a large business, or any large organization, the response to blame by someone fairly high up the pyramid is to try and push it sideways, or more likely, downwards onto the next level below. In fact, the ability of an individual to avoid blame in this way often defines just how important he is within the organization. It's very easy and tempting to do if you're at the top, and so it's heart-warming to see CEOs who fairly and squarely proclaim mea culpa big time. One of these is Michael O'Leary, boss of Ryanair, who candidly admitted that he had "messed up" in making the wrong call about trends in airline fuel prices.

Keeping it clean

In the British Isles and North America there tends to be much emphasis on transparency. Financial statements should tell it "how it is," and there is usually a small army of specialists pouring through the figures to catch out any "creative accounting." If anything goes awry there maybe much finger pointing in the press. Reputations may suffer in the short term. They may also have to pay fines or maybe suffer indignities like being barred from serving as a director in the future or holding fiduciary duties.

There are no really serious consequences—no firing squads, either figuratively or literally, nor sounds of prison doors slamming. Yet, there are exceptions. One of the biggest business scandals hit the headlines in the early 1990s, involving the murky actions of the Guinness Four. They were found guilty and sentenced to between one and five years. Gerald Ronson served six months and Ernest Saunders ten months in an open prison. While all four suffered loss of reputation and decline in wealth from the heady heights they were accustomed to (Jack Lyons was stripped of his knighthood and CBE), none have been reduced to begging in the streets. Ernest Saunders went on to become a much sought-after business consultant, advising firms like Carphone Warehouse.

The trial might never have taken place had Ivan "the Terrible" Boesky's fall from grace in the United States not uncovered his links with the Guinness Four, which were then passed on to the British Department of Trade and Industry.

The whole affair was unpleasant, reflecting a side of the business world which "decent" people hoped didn't exist. While there are quite draconian pieces of legislation on the UK statue book involving things such as fraud, insider dealing, and false accounting, there is a hope that they have a deterrent effect. The United Kingdom may represent a Guilt Society, where the fear of guilt is used to maintain social cohesion and respect for norms—but it is deeply uncomfortable about it. It is as if a red-faced John Bull replies to the assertion in an embarrassed manner with evasive agreement, adding: "We don't like to speak in those terms and anyway guilt's such an unpleasant word isn't it—would you like a cup of tea?"

There is deep unease among government circles at having to take on large companies. This is reflected in the law itself. While it's not uncommon for even the biggest company to get sued, this is a civil case, settled by the payment of financial damages. Bringing a criminal case against a company is an entirely different affair. Dealing with individual criminals is easy—the courts have been doing it for hundreds of years. He or she has an undivided mental space—one mind controlled (hopefully) by one person who takes responsibility for its acts. But you can't apply this to a company or corporation, employing hundreds, maybe thousands of people. Where is its single mind? Does it even have one? Sure, the individual actions of all its managers make up a big chunk of its daily operations, but this is not a single mental entity for the purposes of the law. And what about staff lower down the pyramid? What about contractors? Where do you stop? Even the most centralized business conducted by the most egotistical martinet of a CEO will still have operations across various levels and functional silos that he or she will not know about still less care.

Messing up in America

In the United States failure is treated much more leniently at one level. It is merely the other side of the coin of success. But if the law has been broken, regarding issues such as fraud, false accounting, or insider trading the punishments can be severe. The armory of statute law to prevent illegal practices is very extensive, and unlike in the United Kingdom, a vast plethora of agencies exist at both federal and state level to actively investigate wrongdoing. Blame will be applied, though it may take years and millions of dollars and countless appeals, to make it stick.

And it is not just the government that can call business to account. The United States has long allowed Class Action and Mass Action lawsuits, the former where a plaintiff is allowed to bring an action on behalf of others, the latter where a group of like-minded litigants join forces. These operate at the civil law level—they can (and do) lead to sizable financial payouts, often blowing big holes in corporate balance sheets, not to say ripping reputations to shreds.

But if somebody is found to have broken the law that's a criminal matter and prison beckons, unless a hotshot legal advocate can be recruited. If convicted you can keep your life but you may have to spend it behind bars. Kenneth Lay, CEO of Enron, had been facing a 40-year prison sentence before he died of a heart attack in July 2006. Others undergo a truly life-changing experience. Ivan Boesky spent two years in jail, was fined $100 million, and barred for life from involvement with the securities industry. Since his liberation he has been a changed man, spending much time in Jewish religious studies. Not that misdoing is the domain of men. Martha Stewart is a particular case in point. Having "atoned," she has again become the darling of the culinary world.

The United States is a fairly well-developed Guilt Society. Feelings of guilt, which need to be both atoned for and punished, are used to solidify social cohesion. Personal feelings of guilt are rarely enough, and are usually backed up by legal means and punishments. Punishments when handed out aren't always enough. The guilty individual may feel a need to atone further, as Boesky has done. Imprisonment and fines are meant to change aberrant behavior. The various prison services have been known for over a century and a half as departments of correction.

Sour milk in China

Let's compare these attitudes with how blame is viewed in China. In September 2008, 6 children died and over 6,000 became sick after consuming powdered milk from some of China's top dairies. A subsequent investigation by food quality watchdogs found that 10 percent of liquid milk from three dairies was contaminated with the toxin melamine, a chemical usually employed in the manufacture of plastics, but which, when added to milk, can give a false impression of higher protein content. In all over a quarter of a million people, became ill. Chinese milk products were withdrawn from sale throughout East Asia.

The authorities' response was swift and severe—but not unusual. The head of the dairy at the center of the scandal, Sanlu, was given a life sentence in addition to a $2.9 million fine. Tian Wenhua was accused of knowingly allowing 900 tons of toxic milk to leave the plant and enter the distribution system, a state of affairs that continued until Sanlu's external partner from New Zealand called a halt to the practice. Two others—a farmer who had manufactured the melamine for mixing with milk, and a milk trader who had then introduced the infected milk into the manufacturing system—were sentenced to a bullet in the back of the neck.

The Chinese legal system is still developing, after years of being dominated by "people's justice." There are new laws regarding food safety. But behind these lie a notion that seems remarkably individualistic by Western standards. The faults of an organization can and will be traced down to an individual or individuals who will be punished severely for any transgressions. For a traditional shame society, China is displaying the classic signs of migrating to a guilt society. Those who do wrong must handle the guilt and must make amends for it. Interestingly, at the beginning of 2009 many of the firms involved in the scandal sent a mass text message admitting their wrongdoing and begging for forgiveness.

Blame in Japan—taking it personally

Japan is a society that places a lot of emphasis on the collective. Conformity is the name of the game and speaking out or acting ostentatiously isn't just wrong, but is viewed as practically obscene. Self-respect is gained not by doing what's right or wrong, but what society expects. But when it comes to shame it is always felt by the individual. It is bound up with feelings of disgust and self-loathing at having violated the norms of the collective. Shame at personal failings is used to maintain social cohesion; it cannot be lessened or removed by confessing or coming clean. This may mean the ultimate personal sacrifice—suicide, a very individualist response to social pressures.

For years Western attitudes toward Japanese responses to bad news have been dominated by the spectacle of *hara-kiri*, and "Death with honour is better than life with dishonour" and so on. This can be called the Madame Butterfly syndrome. As a term hara-kiri isn't used in Japan—what we understand by it comes under the name *seppuku* (literally stomach cutting). In the past seppuku was only open to members of the Samurai military elite. It was particularly common among military leaders who failed to win victories or who did not want to become prisoners-of-war. It naturally migrated to those Japanese bosses who saw their companies as armies manned by thousands of loyal *sarariman* (salarymen).

Japanese business law is heavily influenced by American models, but at times of financial difficulties suicide is still the preferred way of dealing with irresolvable problems for which a CEO feels personally responsible.

Since the end of the Second World War, seppuku has become democratized—anyone who could afford the necessary kit of an authentic seventeenth-century sword could do it. Other methods of putting an end to fortune's slings and arrows, like jumping out of windows or overdoses are also alarmingly common. More complicated is jumping in front of a train, because some insensitive rail companies have been known to bring a suicide's family to court for possible damages to train engines, something they are more likely to do if they feel confident of gaining financially.

Heads I win, tails you lose

Blame's role in various cultures can be explored, but it is only fair to point out that there are some countries whose attitude to blame is quite simple. It's never their fault. This can be linked to a simplistic reading of recent history, where the country and its people have suffered at the hands of external, colonialist aggressors. So the locals can do no wrong. It's always the outsider's fault.

In a North African country a natural gas processing plant was operated jointly by the national oil company and a Canadian multinational. Many of the middle management and supervisory staff were locals, though in the opinion of the plant engineer they wouldn't work "to save their lives." Most were employed just to keep the ministry happy. Amongst their duties was to monitor the temperature of water used as a coolant. On one occasion the water's temperature nearly reached boiling point, causing an emergency shut down. The supervisors, whose job it had been to keep an eye on the dials had been distracted: they were watching a football match. All this was known to the plant's manager, a South Korean, but he also knew he couldn't even issue the mildest reprimand. Two days later he received a high-powered delegation from the ministry, informing him that a "thorough" investigation of the plant shutdown had found that he personally was to blame. He was handed a document to sign, in which he confessed his "faults" against the host country and its people, for all of which he begged the local's forgiveness. He signed and got on the next plane to Seoul, never to return.

This simplistic assessment of blame can also be found in another Arab country—Saudi Arabia. Many an ex-pat who has ever had the misfortune to be involved in a traffic accident in Saudi can tell how the crash is always the foreigner's fault. The reasoning is usually that the accident wouldn't—couldn't have occurred if the foreigner hadn't come to Saudi Arabia in the first place.

Stock markets drive global corporations. These corporations distribute global goods and services in both global and local markets. Such breath of responsibility makes being held accountable a global phenomenon. The skill of the leader is to create a positive culture of accountability without being sucked into the blame game.

Ask Yourself

- Is your organization's a shame or a guilt culture?
- How do you manage different attitudes to blame in other stakeholders you deal with?
- Do you hold others accountable without searching for a scapegoat?

So there you have it: our 21 shots of global leadership. It is not a final list, of course. It never could be, but it represents our experiences of living, working, and leading in a global business world.

In the end, we believe that reach, capacity to roll out, and level of readiness are fundamental to being a successful global executive. We also believe that for all the talk of a flat and homogenous world, the opposite is true. The world is more heterogeneous than ever. The many and varied cultural influences, customs, and attitudes have a long and meaningful history and are very real to every leader's local constituents.

Indeed, every one of us is both global and local depending on who we meet on any given day, or hour of the day, and the issue under discussion. One's own emotions can be globally mature—seeing the total picture on the one hand and being able to stand above the local context—and yet when faced with different challenges or people can be very local, myopic, and defensive. In the final analysis, then, we are neither local nor global: we are both but untidily so.

So let us go back to where we started. When Andrew was drinking rice wine with the minister, the real test was not of his supposed manhood but of being sufficiently trusted to maintain a logical and impressive conversation while under the pressure of being distracted by local rituals, other people's emotions and anxieties and particularly the rice wine.

Andrew showed that he could pursue sharp dialog while being sensitive to the guests at the table—even when they could no longer hold their liquor. The trust being tested was not: "Do I trust you as a person," but more "Do I trust your capacity to handle pressure and engage with others and still put forward an impressive and penetrating case that could win the attention of all those concerned? Is this someone I want on my side when the chips are down."

All cultures have similar tests and trials. Some are more direct, open, and functional; others more subtle and intricate. In the end, though, it is the leader's ability to navigate these cultural chicanes and come through these examinations of their character and intent with flying colors that determines their ability to function effectively as global leaders.

Good luck!

Notes

1. Kakabadse, Andrew and Kakabadse Nada (2008) *Leading the Board: The Six Disciplines of World Class Chairmen*, Palgrave Macmillan, London.
2. Ibid.
3. Ibid.
4. Ibid.
5. Drucker, P. (1974) *Management Tasks, Responsibilities, Practices,* Harper & Row, New York.
6. Babbage, Charles (1989) *The Works of Charles Babbage.* Edited by Martin Campbell-Kelly, London: William Pickering; Frederick Winslow Taylor (1911) *The Principles of Scientific Management,* Harper & Row, New York.
7. Kepner, C. and Tregoe, B. (1981) *The New Rational Manager*, John Martin, London.
8. Interesting takes on decision-making can be found in the following: Dearlove, Des (1996) *Key Management Decisions*, Financial Times Prentice Hall; French, Simon (1988) *Decision Theory: An Introduction to the Mathematics of Rationality*, Ellis Horwood and John Wiley, New York; Keeney, Ralph, L. (1992) *Value-Focused Thinking: A Path to Creative Decision Making*, Harvard University Press; Richards, Max D. and Greenlaw, Paul S. (1966) *Management Decision Making*, Richard D. Irwin Inc.; and Yates, J. Frank (1990) *Judgement and Decision Making*, Prentice Hall, New Jersey. Richards and Greenlaw, and Yates.
9. Stewart-Allen, A. and Denslow, L. (2002) *Working with Americans: How to Build Profitable Business Relationships*, Pearson, Harlow, UK.
10. Machiavelli, Niccolò (1984) *The Prince*, Bantam, New York.
11. Kim, W. Chan and Mauborgne, Renee (2007) *Blue Ocean Strategy*, Harvard Press, Boston.
12. Kakabadse, Andrew and Kakabadse, Nada (2008) *Leading the Board: The Six Disciplines of World Class Chairmen*, Palgrave Macmillan, London, p. 52.
13. Ibid., p. 110.

14. Howard Gardner interviewed by Des Dearlove can be seen at www.thinkers50. com.

15. Kakabadse, Andrew and Kakabadse, Nada (2008) *Leading the Board: The Six Disciplines of World Class Chairmen*, Palgrave Macmillan, London, p. 72.

16. Ibid., p. 71.

17. Ibid., p. 74.

18. Kakabadse, Andrew and Kakabadse, Nada (2008) *Leading the Board: The Six Disciplines of World Class Chairmen*, Palgrave Macmillan, London.

19. Ibid., p. 83.

Arnold, D. J. and Quelch, J. A. "New strategies in emerging markets," *Sloan Management Review*, 40(1), 1998.

Bruner, J. S., *Acts of Meaning*, Harvard University Press, 1990.

Charkham, J. P., *Keeping Good Company: A Study of Corporate Governance in Five Countries*, Oxford Paperbacks, 1995.

Collins, J. and Porras, J., *Built to Last: Successful Habits of Visionary Companies*, Random House Business Books, 1998.

De Geus, A., *The Living Company: Habits for Survival in a Turbulent Business Environment*, Harvard Business School Press, 2002.

De Smet, A., Loch, Mark, and Schaninger, Bill, "Anatomy of a healthy corporation," *McKinsey Quarterly*, May 2007.

Deanne N. D. H., "What indeed do managers do? Some reflections on Rosemary Stewart's work," *The Leadership Quarterly,* 14, 2003.

Dearlove, D. and Crainer, S., "What happened to real debate among corporate directors?" *The Conference Board Review*, November 2007.

Earley, P. C. and Peterson, R. S., "The elusive cultural chameleon: Cultural intelligence as a new approach to intercultural training for the global manger," *Academy of Management Learning and Education*, 3(1), 2004.

Green, S., *Manager's Guide to the Sarbanes-Oxley Act: Improving Internal Controls to Prevent Fraud,* John Wiley & Sons, 2004.

Green, S. and Hassan, F., Immelt, J. Marks, M. and Meiland, D., "In search of global leaders," *Harvard Business Review*, 81(6), 2003.

Heenan, D. and Bennis, W., *Co-Leaders: Who Wields the Real Power in Organizations Today?* John Wiley & Sons, 1999.

Kakabadse, A., *The Wealth Creators: Top People, Top Teams and Executive Best Practice*, Kogan Page, 1991.

Kakabadse, A. and Kakabadse, N., *Essence of Leadership* (1st Edition), Thompson Publishing, 1999.

Kakabadse, A. and Kakabadse, N., *The Geopolitics Of Governance: The Impact Of Contrasting Philosophies*, Palgrave, 2001.

Kakabadse, A. and Kakabadse, N., *Leading the Board*, Palgrave Macmillan, 2008.

Kakabadse, A. and Kakabadse, N. (Eds.), *CSR in Practice: Delving Deep*, Palgrave Macmillan, 2006.

Kakabadse, A., Kakabadse, N., and Kalu, K. (Eds.), *Citizenship: A Reality Far from Ideal*, Palgrave Macmillan, 2009.

Katz, D. and Kahn, R. L., *The Social Psychology of Organizations*, John Wiley & Sons, 1966.

Khurana, R., *Searching for a Corporate Savior: The Irrational Quest for Charismatic CEOs*, Princeton University Press, 2002.

Lawrence, Peter A., *Management in Western Europe*, Macmillan Business, 2000.

Lorsch, J. W. and MacIver, E., *Pawns or Potentates: The Reality of America's Corporate Boards*, Harvard Business School Press, 1989.

Marx, E., *Route to the Top: A Transatlantic Comparison of Top Business Leaders*, Heidrick and Struggles, 2008.

Merton, R. K., *Social Theory and Social Structure* (Revised Edition), Free Press, 1957.

Monks, R. A. G. and Minow, N., *Corporate Governance* (3rd Edition), Blackwell Publishing, 2003.

Nadler, D. A., Behan, B. A., and Nadler, M. B., *Building Better Boards: A Blueprint for Effective Governance*, Jossey-Bass, 2006.

Richmond, B., "The thinking' in systems thinking: How can we make it easier?" *The Systems Thinker*, 8(2), 1997.

Thomson, P., Lloyd, T., and Graham J., *Woman's Place in the Boardroom*, Palgrave Macmillan, 2008.

Watts, A., *Tao: The Watercourse Way,* Pantheon Books, 1975.

Wibbeke, E. S., *Global Business Leadership*, Butterworth-Heinemann, 2008.